THE GOD WHO RIOTS

PRAISE FOR *THE GOD WHO RIOTS: TAKING BACK THE RADICAL JESUS*

"Damon Garcia is a narrative theologian who has spent the past few years listening to the people protesting for liberation in the United States. His insights into scripture are profound and desperately needed. In a time of enormous social upheaval, we need voices like Garcia who are prepared to embrace a world where the formerly poor and powerless lead the way to a more just world. This is a must-read for any pastor or minister who hopes to hear the message of the unheard in our society."

—D. L. Mayfield, author of *The Myth of the American Dream* and *Unruly Saint: Dorothy Day's Radical Vision and Its Challenge for Our Times*

"The God of Christians has been many different things to many people. Often used to justify injustice and abuse, this God has left a sour taste in the mouths of the most marginalized amongst us. But there is also *The God Who Riots*, the God who Damon speaks in this book, a God who invites us to disrupt systems and create heaven on earth."

—Jo Luehmann, host of *The Living Room with Jo Luehmann* and author of the Decolonizing Traditional Christianity devotional

"Following Jesus is costly, and our work today is to count the cost of what it really means to follow a Brown Palestinian Jew. Living in Babylon and resisting the acceleration of the empire religion of white ChristoFascism, we must seek to get our hands dirty with the everyday and riot alongside God who cares first for the underside of history."

—Robyn Henderson-Espinoza, PhD, author of *Body Becoming* and *Activist Theology*

"In an age of capitalism crises and encroaching climate catastrophe, the work of a genuinely liberatory theology has never been more urgent. Damon Garcia's work provides a much-needed vision of the real good news that lies at the heart of the gospel."

—Jon Greenaway, writer and academic, @thelitcritguy

"Damon equips us with the kind of theological paradigm needed to sustain an authentic faith in these times. His words are relevant and accessible to the privileged, the marginalized, and everyone in between. His offering is truly a welcome addition to the canon of liberation theology."

—Rev. Aurelia Dávila Pratt, author of *A Brown Girl's Epiphany*

"Damon Garcia shares the real radical message of Jesus—a message where love and liberation are as bright as a burning prison. Wherever you are on your faith journey—whether you're new to Christianity, deconstructing, or a lifelong Christian—this book is for those who want to follow the true radical Jesus."

—Mason Mennenga, YouTuber and podcast host of *A People's Theology*

"With the skill and enthusiasm of your favorite teacher from high school, Garcia takes weighty and serious topics and makes them accessible, learnable, and immediate. If you've wanted to learn about the liberation, decolonization, and abolitionist streams of Christian faith but didn't know where to start, let *The God Who Riots* invite you in and accompany you toward a radical faith."

—Kevin Nye, author of *Grace Can Lead Us Home: A Christian Call to End Homelessness*

"Often, Christians imagine Jesus as an apolitical figure. But drawing from both Christian scripture and tradition, Garcia introduces us to Christ from a different angle—Jesus isn't leading us toward otherworldly salvation, but instead struggles with us for our liberation from all manner of oppression."

—Matt Bernico, The Magnificast

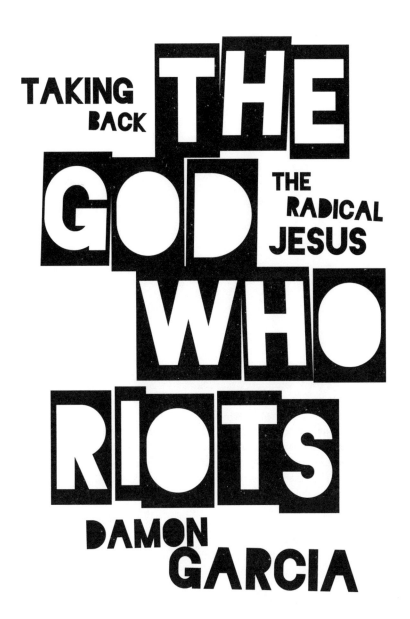

TAKING BACK THE GOD WHO RIOTS

THE RADICAL JESUS

DAMON GARCIA

Broadleaf Books
Minneapolis

Cover image: serts/iStock
Cover design: Faceout Studios

Print ISBN: 978-1-5064-8037-4
eBook ISBN: 978-1-5064-8038-1

To the Hallway (2012–2014)

Our conversations about faith and life were the beginning of the joyful and difficult journey that led me to this book.

CONTENTS

INTRODUCTION

I've always suspected that Jesus was way more radical than the Christians I grew up around could comprehend.

A few years ago, I met with the associate pastors at my church and nervously confessed to them that I didn't feel comfortable inviting other young adults to service on Sundays. I was the youth and young adults minister, so it was literally my job to bring young people into that church, but it became a burden.

The year was 2017. My peers were talking about Trump's travel ban on Muslim countries, immigration, police brutality, white supremacy, and trans rights. Throughout the year there were also Black Lives Matter protests, women's marches, and teacher strikes. And yet, every Sunday morning we ignored all that.

The associate pastors listened to me as I explained this, and responded, "I don't think there's as many people thinking about all that stuff as you think there are."

I left that church about a month later. But leaving that church didn't feel like I was leaving Jesus. It felt like I was following Jesus into something bigger.

I had come to realize that it was wrong to remain neutral on so many points of injustice. We claimed to be a community that followed Jesus, but I don't know what kind of Jesus this was. The Jesus of the Bible empowered people to confront injustice, not avoid it.

My favorite Jesus story is a scene a few days before Jesus is crucified where he enters the temple's outer courts and shuts the place down. Jesus flips over the tables of those selling sacrificial animals and pours out their coins on the ground. With a whip he drives out the people and animals and won't allow anyone to carry anything through the temple. He then uses the place to teach and accuses the priests of turning a house of prayer into a den of robbers.

A den of robbers is not where people are robbed. A den of robbers is where robbers hide, expecting to be safe. Jesus uses this temple demonstration to accuse the religious authorities of hiding behind their religion to avoid confronting the injustice going on outside of the temple. Today, we all know Christians who hide behind their religion to avoid confronting injustice, so this demonstration is more relevant than ever.

Again and again, the God of the Bible chooses the side of the oppressed. Jesus embodies this decisiveness. Jesus said the spirit of the Lord anointed him "to let the oppressed go free."[1] This is the purpose of Jesus's ministry. The language of choosing sides is uncomfortable in our highly divisive times. Often we are trying to escape "us vs. them" stories. In our attempt to combat our divisiveness, we often prioritize harmony over justice. However, this only prolongs the injustice that is at the root of our divisions.

Religious organizations' priority for harmony over justice has led to various critiques of religion over the centuries. It's why Karl Marx called religion the opium of the masses, imagining flowers over our chains. It's why we may love spirituality but get really uncomfortable around people who seem to over-spiritualize things. It's why we roll our eyes at people who claim that the solution to suffering is simply a change of perspective, while ignoring the oppression that continues no matter how we perceive it.

Justice requires us to choose sides. Even love requires us to choose sides. And choosing the side of the oppressed requires us to fight for what the oppressed fight for. People need others to share their struggle.

This is the objective of the incarnation. God is embodied in Jesus, a poor and powerless child, who grows up to build a movement in solidarity with the poor and powerless unto his death. Through Jesus, God chooses sides. It is only through the poor and powerless that salvation becomes available to everyone. Supporting the poor and powerless in their struggle to free themselves is how we all get free.

In the spirit of this incarnational sensibility, the American Christian socialist Eugene Debs famously said,

> I recognized my kinship with all living beings, and I made up my mind that I was not one bit better than the meanest on earth. I said then, and I say now, that while there is a lower class, I am in it, and while there is a criminal element I am of it, and while there is a soul in prison, I am not free.[2]

Choosing the side of the underclass is a deep impulse throughout Christian history, but it's never been the most popular expression of Christianity in the world. In my search for a more liberative Christianity I discovered liberation theology, which is a major influence on my faith today. Liberation theology was formulated in Latin America in the 1960s out of a commitment to "the preferential option for the poor." The sentiment behind this slogan was that God always chooses the side of the poor in their struggle for freedom from oppression, so the church should too. The only reason liberation theology had to develop as a distinct interpretive lens is because of the history of the church choosing the side of the rich and powerful again and again until it was impossible to imagine or recognize a mainstream Christianity that chooses the side of the poor and powerless.

In spite of Christianity's corrupt history, there has always persisted a stream within Christianity that chooses the side of the poor and powerless. One of my heroes, St. Francis of Assisi, started an order of friars called the Lesser Brothers, who were committed to poverty and charity. His motivation was to serve every need of the poorest people in society to the extent that the Brothers had fewer material resources than those they served. They tapped into that incarnational sensibility and viscerally understood the significance of Jesus saying, "Whatever you did to the least of these, you did to me."[3] He did this during the Crusades, in the same country as the pope.

We can either use our faith to empower us to transform the world or use our faith to justify the world as it is. Our faith often operates as one form or the other, even if we are not aware of it. Both of these forms of faith live within us, always at tension. And both of these forms of faith have shaped our history, always at tension.

This book is about that tension.

Many of us are more familiar with the ways Christianity has been used to suppress change, which is why many of us have a complicated relationship with religion. You are not alone. This is my story too. And my faith opened up in new ways when I discovered the stream of Christianity that empowers the work of liberation, even when it requires fighting injustice within the Christian tradition itself.

This book is written from a Christian perspective, and is mostly about Christianity, not because I believe Christianity is superior to other religions, or that Christians have special access to God that non-Christians don't have. Rather, since I grew up in Christianity, it is my responsibility to reclaim my own religious tradition to empower myself toward liberation. It is the responsibility of people of other religious traditions to reclaim theirs in their own way.

The Christian faith begins with Jesus as the point of entry to God. Jesus uniquely shows us what God is like. And it is through Jesus's riotous demonstration in the temple that we experience the God who riots. This God is manifest in all kinds of places we may not expect. And as I look at modern-day riots, protests, strikes, and all other forms of direct action toward liberation, I am compelled to bear witness to the God who riots, continuing to empower people in the work of liberation.

This God chooses sides in our struggle. In response to injustice, this God riots alongside us, within us, and through us.

1

SAVED FROM WHAT?

Jesus was arrested and executed because of the trouble he was stirring up in Jerusalem.

The story of Jesus shutting down the temple describes a planned demonstration and a riot, complete with property destruction, looting, and social unrest. This usually isn't the first image that comes to mind when people think about Jesus. Many of my friends, both Christian and non-Christian, didn't even know this story was in the Bible. Some of my other friends, both Christian and non-Christian, share my love for this story. I've heard people say they don't support Christianity but have a soft spot for Jesus, and this story is one of the main reasons they do.

A reason we find this story so compelling is because we are typically familiar with religious people—especially Christians—being resistant to change. And yet in this story, one of the most famous religious figures in history is fighting for change. Jesus witnesses injustice and moves against it. Every movement against injustice throughout the last century has been met with suppression from those who resist change, and that suppression has often come from Christians. We've seen this in the fight for women's liberation, Black liberation, gay liberation, and onward. Jesus wants change. And he's executed for it.

HOW WE CHANGE

Religion has empowered people to fight for a new world, and religion has also justified the institutions of the current world. Religion has served these two roles throughout history. Religion can also empower us to change as individuals, or it can hinder us from changing.

Every time I've gone through a significant change in my life, my Christian faith was a part of the process. My faith has always contained this tension. Part of my faith empowered me to change, while another part held me back from changing.

There's a story I relate to a lot in Acts 10 about the apostle Peter going through this kind of conflict in the midst of change. Peter fell into a trance while deep in prayer and saw a vision of "something like a large sheet" coming down from heaven, filled with "all kinds of four-footed creatures and reptiles and birds of the air." Peter then heard a voice say, "Get up, Peter; kill and eat." Peter, being faithful to traditional Jewish dietary laws, responded, "By no means, Lord; for I have never eaten anything that is profane or unclean."

The amusing part of this story is Peter telling God he can't eat anything unclean because God told him he can't. Peter has a God-given opportunity for change, but before he can embrace it, he has to confront his conception of God that refuses to change.

The voice from heaven then tells Peter, "What God has made clean, you must not call profane." Peter awoke from his trance, and while he was trying to figure out the meaning of this vision, he was invited to talk about Jesus to non-Jews for the first time.

Then he got it.

Peter grew up seeing everyone outside his people group as unclean, and in this moment, God called them all clean. In order to embrace this new way of seeing the world, Peter had to embrace a new conception of God. His previous conception of God helped him get to where he was. Now it was time to let it go.

This is how growth works. A new way of life becomes desirable when you experience the constraints of your current way of life. Then the conditions of a new way of life emerge as a solution to the problems caused by the constraints of your current way of life. While you would prefer to peacefully transition to your new way of life, this process is always met with conflict. This conflict comes from the part of you that has previously benefited from the conditions of your current way of life.

And yet, there are other parts of you that have experienced the constraints of your current way of life and cause you to become unhealthy—emotionally unhealthy, or perhaps physically unhealthy. The process of transitioning to a new way of life begins with your dissatisfaction. Initially you try to ignore the dissatisfied part of yourself because the part that benefits from your current way of life has a louder voice within you. That voice gets quieter and quieter as you become more and more dissatisfied, and the dissatisfied voice becomes louder within you.

Inevitably, the dissatisfied part of yourself wins this conflict, and you develop a new way of life. This process is never a singular moment toward a final state of maturity. This process happens again and again throughout your life, beginning again when you inevitably experience the constraints of your new way of life.

GETTING SAVED

My faith has always empowered me to listen to the dissatisfied voice within me. I've always believed this is what the Christian life is supposed to look like.

Embracing change always seemed more Christian than resisting change, even when I was a young child.

One Wednesday night during my childhood I was attending a kids' church service, and I saw another kid I recognized from my elementary school named Richard. Richard had been mean to my friends and me, so I was shocked to see him at church. From my childish perspective I assumed the nice kids at school were probably Christian, and the mean kids were probably the furthest thing from it.

At the end of the service, the minister asked who wanted to accept Jesus into their heart, or something like that, and I saw Richard raise his hand. Once again, I was shocked, but I was mostly happy because I assumed this meant Richard would start being a lot nicer to my friends and me at school.

The next day during P.E. class, as we were standing on our numbers on the blacktop, I told my friends the news. "Richard got saved last night!" I blurted out.

To my surprise, they had no idea what I was talking about. "Saved from what?" they asked.

I was immediately stumped. "Saved" was the word my church used when someone became a Christian. I thought my friends would understand what I meant, and elaborating felt impossibly difficult. I just knew he was saved, and it was good news for us. I couldn't explain why I thought that way though, and I definitely couldn't explain what "saved" meant, or what "saved people" are saved *from*, exactly.

I look back at that moment and recognize that I certainly understood that "getting saved" had something to do with some sort of personal transformation.

I probably had this impression from observing my parents' own personal transformations. They started going to church when I was two years old. They had both been drug addicts and alcoholics, and my dad had been in and out of prison. One day they both decided they wanted to change their lives. My mom's sister had recently started going to church, so my parents joined a church.

The spiritual teachings of that community gave them a sense of dignity they didn't have before. Knowing they were loved and cared for by God and by that supportive community empowered them to live differently. They were saved, and in this circumstance, they were saved from the destructive coping mechanisms they had developed while they were struggling through life on their own.

They were saved from something, yes, but they were also saved *for* something.

Many Christians use the word "saved" today to refer to their souls being saved from hell. And yet, the idea that Richard's soul might be saved from hell wasn't on my mind at all when I was standing there on the blacktop trying to explain to my friends what "saved" meant.

When I looked at my parents, I knew "getting saved" looked like getting saved from the destruction taking place right here and right now. They recovered from the effects of that destruction by living differently in a loving and supportive community. They were saved, but it had nothing to do with their souls or an afterlife.

In the Hebrew Bible, or the Old Testament, salvation is first conceptualized through the experience of the ancient Israelites escaping slavery in Egypt. This is such a defining moment that, throughout the rest of the scripture, God is frequently named as "the God who brought the Israelites out of Egypt." Much later in the story, Israel is defeated. The Israelites are taken captive by Babylon and exiled from their home. They cry out to God to save them from exile just like God saved them from Egypt, and God sends prophets promising their salvation. Salvation is about the collective fate of a nation. Salvation is about an actual experience of physical liberation during *this* life.

When we get to the New Testament, the concept of salvation becomes more personal. There is still talk of salvation as collective, but the first Christians viewed their collective liberation as contingent on our individual participation in the work of liberation. The first Christians still longed for a larger collective liberation led by God, but their unique message was that it was going to require our participation as well. For the early Christians, salvation looked like a personal decision to transform our way of being in the world, working out our own salvation "with fear and trembling."[1]

In Acts 2, Peter preached to a crowd, "Save yourselves from this corrupt generation."[2] Peter was inviting people to a new way of being in the world. The Christian movement was called The Way before its members were called Christians. The first Christians were distinguished first and foremost by the way they took care of one another in community. Saving oneself looked like choosing the side of the oppressed as they struggled for salvation from their oppression. This was very different from other movements that preached about a coming Messiah.

Many people besides Jesus claimed to be the Messiah in the first century, sent by God to liberate the people of Israel and establish the kingdom of God. Most of them were also executed on crosses by Rome. Whenever a Messiah was executed, their followers decided they were wrong about who the Messiah was and went home to wait for another one. But something different happened among Jesus's followers after his execution. They decided they were wrong about *what* the Messiah was, not *who*.

Then they claimed to be the body of the Messiah, or the body of Christ. *Christ* is the Greek rendering of the Hebrew term *mashiach*, which means "anointed one." The church was a community of anointed ones. They understood that the salvation of the oppressed could only happen through uniting as one body in that struggle for salvation. They claimed that the resurrection of Christ was only the first fruits of a greater resurrection taking place through the continual embodiment of Christ in the lives of this new community.

The fact that the early Christian community made these claims can be confirmed historically. The debate is around what made them shift their perspective. Was it really their experience of Jesus coming back to life? Was it visions they had of Jesus? Was it a collective reinterpretation of the teachings of Jesus years after his death? The answer to that question is a matter of faith, but no matter the reason for changing their minds, the radical shift in the way Jesus's followers talked about the Messiah, or the Christ, is historical.

This shift in seeing themselves as the body of Christ transformed the way they lived. That's the part that has always inspired me the most.

When we read in the book of Acts about the first Christians being "saved," we read about a unique community of people who were transforming people's lives.

> All who believed were together and had all things in common; they would sell their possessions and goods and distribute the proceeds to all, as any had need. Day by day, as they spent much time together in the temple, they broke bread at home and ate their food with glad and generous hearts, praising God and having the goodwill of all the people. And day by day the Lord added to their number those who were being saved.[3]

When you join a community like this, you must have been compelled within yourself to answer the question, *Who is making a better world here? Rome? Or Jesus? Whose side do I choose?*

Some 2,000 years later, my parents decided to join this movement.

WIDENING

When I was 18, I felt called into ministry, and after much stubborn refusal I realized I found a lot of fulfillment whenever I preached and taught people about these ideas. I found a new passion and dreamed of being a pastor one day. So I enrolled in a ministry training program in my denomination and took Bible college classes.

The more I studied, however, the more I found myself agreeing with Christian perspectives that were beyond the boundaries of what my denomination considered the right interpretation of the Christian faith. Within the evangelical corner of Christianity I grew up in, I had suddenly become a heretic.

The word *heretic* comes from the Greek, *hairetikós*, which simply means "able to choose." Historically the word has been used to describe Christians who had dissented from the church's official doctrines and dogmas. And yet, my journey into heresy felt less like a dissent from historical church teaching, and more like a consistent realization that contemporary American evangelicalism had dissented from historical church teaching to a surprising extent. I discovered many evangelical doctrines that were only a couple hundred years old, while my church taught me that they were what the early Christians believed.

I didn't have an issue with evangelical teachings being new. I'm fine believing in ideas developed in contemporary settings. I'm also not particularly passionate about believing in the oldest—or most original—Christian ideas either. My issue was that contemporary evangelical teachings were taught as the only way to interpret the Christian faith and were tied to the faith of the early Christians in a way that totally obscured church history. I knew there was way more out there.

So my journey of dissent felt more like a loyal commitment to discover truth, which naturally placed me outside the boundaries they wanted me to stay inside of. This journey always felt like a widening. I confronted the limitations of a particular perspective of faith and then widened to a new one. And I just kept allowing this to happen.

One day I could no longer in good conscience and conviction call myself a Pentecostal. And then one day I could no longer call myself an evangelical. And then I could no longer call myself a Protestant. These are various branches within the larger Christian tradition. Pentecostals are a type of evangelical. Evangelicals are a type of Protestant. And Protestants are a type of Christian. So eventually, the only thing I felt I could authentically call myself was a Christian.

Even though my beliefs and values had progressed outside of my denomination's boundaries, I tried to work around our differences for years. I dropped out of Bible college, but I started working at the church I grew up in as a youth and young adults minister. It was during the process of getting my pastoral license, when I looked at the list of questions I would have to answer in my licensing interview, that I knew I couldn't make it work anymore. I knew I couldn't answer their questions the way they wanted me to while still being honest.

So I left. I lost so many friends and opportunities, but I couldn't risk losing my integrity by staying.

My Christian faith led me out of the community that initially taught me about that faith.

My story is far from unique. This is how everyone goes through change. We confront the constraints of our current way of life and develop a new one to solve the problems of those constraints. Even in the midst of our diverse beliefs, values, and identities, the process of change is similar for all of us. This process of change even extends to massive changes in history.

HOW THE WORLD CHANGES

This is how historical change works. A new world becomes desirable when people experience the constraints of the current world, just like a new way of life becomes desirable when you personally run into the constraints of your current way of life. Then the conditions of a new world emerge as a solution to the problems caused by the constraints of the previous world. While it is always preferable to peacefully replace the conditions of the current world with a new one, this process is always met with conflict. That conflict comes from those who significantly benefit from the conditions of the current world—those with power.

Those without power are always the first ones to experience the constraints of the conditions of the current world as a result of poverty and discrimination. The process of transitioning to a new world begins with these people's dissatisfaction. Initially the constraints are ignored because not everyone else has experienced them yet. As the current world remains unchanged, more and more people begin to experience its constraints. As more and more people have this experience, they become stronger by uniting with others who share the same experience.

Inevitably, the dissatisfied people of society organize, protest, revolt, and win this conflict. Then they develop a new world. This process is never a singular moment toward a final state of utopia. This process happens again and again throughout history, beginning again when people inevitably experience the constraints of the new world.

As we listen to that dissatisfied voice within ourselves and are compelled toward personal change, we begin to listen to the dissatisfied voices within society as well and are compelled toward societal change.

Nowadays I often interact with people who grew up in conservative Christian environments, then left them behind, and then somehow found themselves involved in radical activism inspired by an anti-fascist, anti-racist, and anti-capitalist vision. A lot of these people tell me they still feel a connection to the Jesus they were taught about when they were younger and, in fact, even feel like it was Jesus who led them into radical politics. This describes my own journey as well.

I got here because of my Christian upbringing, not as a rejection of it. Even as a child, when I heard that Richard got "saved," I knew that becoming a Christian meant you would live in the world in a different way. Sure, we could have a discussion about what happens metaphysically when someone is saved, but I'm not as interested in that conversation—partly because if God is doing something special with my soul, that's God's business, not mine. I'm more interested in what the Christian faith means for how we live our day-to-day lives right here and right now. That's the part we have some control over.

In a world where religion is typically used to suppress change within individuals and within history, Jesus followed a desire for change within himself *and* within the world. And as a man who uniquely embodied God in the world, Jesus reflects this desire for change within

God as well. This is why we love the story of Jesus rioting in the temple.

Religion has always been used to empower people to change themselves and the world. And religion has also been used to suppress change. These two forms of faith are always in tension. In order to live out our faith in the world in a more healthy and responsible way, we must understand this tension.

2

AN ALTERNATIVE TO YOUR DEHUMANIZATION

When I was 19, I started a Bible study called the Hallway for young adults where we could explore our faith and express our doubts and questions. I taught the Bible and led discussions for the first time in this group, so from the beginning my approach to ministry was shaped by a desire to make space for spiritual misfits.

We fully accepted one another with all our doubts and vulnerabilities, allowing us to experience a loving community in a way we hadn't encountered. The unique support and encouragement we practiced for each other had a bigger impact on each of us than any of my teachings. The love from that group of friends transformed me.

As the group grew, I sensed that my beliefs and values were becoming exceedingly divergent from most of the conservative Christians we knew. This terrified me.

I became overcome with anxiety about how my relationships would be affected by my shifting beliefs. So one day I asked my friends if they would still be my friend if I ever became a heretic. Looking back now, I'm embarrassed by how earnestly I asked such a ridiculous question. But the stakes felt very real at the time. They said of course. And that freed me to keep on growing.

Over the years some of those friends distanced themselves from me because of our different beliefs but others stuck around. Those relationships taught me a lot about spirituality.

When I think of some of the foundational spiritual experiences I've had in my life, I do not think of any moments of intellectual enlightenment. My journey has always included an endless intellectual evolution, but my foundational spiritual experiences were the moments where I received love and acceptance from people despite the differences in our intellectual positions and beliefs.

Then there were also the moments where I received rejection because of our differences, and those moments were just as foundational for me. Those moments of acceptance were foundational because they showed me what a spiritual life in community is supposed to be like. Those moments of rejection showed me what a spiritual life in community should *not* be like, which gave me the motivation to develop healthier spiritual communities.

Those moments of acceptance were experiences of grace, being loved and accepted just as I am. Grace is what makes a lot of people fall in love with a church community, especially in today's society where authentic community is significantly more difficult to cultivate.

But often, grace enables us to become keenly aware of the lack of grace in our churches as well. Many of us were inspired and empowered by the church's message of unconditional love and grace, until one day we bumped into the boundaries where our church had set conditions on grace. Grace was abruptly snatched away because we didn't act right, or believe right, or talk right.

And so, naturally, we left.

When you build a community based on a message of unconditional love and grace, you shouldn't be surprised when people leave after experiencing a significant lack of love and grace in that community.

I hear stories like this all the time. People leave Christian communities for Christian reasons.

We are raised with a set of values and principles that taught us to love and value people to a radical extent, and then one day we realize we've begun to love and value people even more than our church is willing to.

We are given the tools to grow, and then we hit the ceiling.

If we are taught that we are holy beings deserving of love and justice, then we will not tolerate being used and abused in *any* environment, even if that environment is the community that taught us about love and justice in the first place. As Rabbi Abraham Joshua Heschel said, "Hypocrisy, rather than heresy is the cause of spiritual decay."[1]

THE WAY WE VALUE EVERYTHING

Religion has always functioned as an alternative method of valuation.

We typically assign value to everything conditionally. A pen is valuable so long as it has ink. A house is valuable so long as it's capable of adequately providing shelter. An object is valuable so long as it can be used. So we naturally can get caught up in seeing people as valuable so long as they prove to be useful.

Religion does something different. Religion assigns unconditional value. Religious communities claim a thing or a person is valuable simply because of their essence, not their usefulness.

The evolution of religion is driven by the way religion assigns value. Religion has been used to justify an unequal distribution of power and resources by valuing some over others, and religion has also been used to empower people to abolish these unjust systems because their religion teaches them that they're *way* more valuable. Religion evolves because the oppressed reshape the religion of their oppressors in order to empower their struggle for liberation, and in turn the oppressors reshape the religion in order to sustain their oppression. Religion has always served these two roles because this is how religion evolves. It cannot be reduced to one or the other. Both expressions are always at tension with one another as we all evolve.

We must acknowledge these two forms of religion if we choose to be religious today. Will we use our religion to justify the ways we are devalued in society? Or will we use religion to resist all the ways we are devalued?

In our current capitalist society, an alternative method of valuation is needed more than ever.

Under a capitalist economic system, everything is turned into a product to be bought and sold. A product's value is no longer determined by its usefulness. Now, a product's value is measured by its exchange value, or rather how much money it could make in a system where the sole motive is profit. Naturally, the value of humans is reduced in this way too. Our usefulness is measured by how much money we make for businesses with our labor.

This has horrendous effects on the way we see ourselves.

The constant effort to prove our value through work affects every part of our lives. In our relationships, we do things, say things, buy things, and act in ways that will make others perceive us as valuable enough to be loved.

Humans cannot be reduced in this way. Humans are useful, yes, but we are also beautiful, underneath all our efforts. Beauty transcends usefulness.

I'm not talking about looks. I'm talking about the beauty that is revealed through the entirety of our being. This beauty is inherent. Your beauty exists because *you* exist. Beauty causes immediate delight in the person who perceives that beauty. That delight is not caused by any sense of usefulness or gain. That delight is caused by the mere existence of that beautiful subject. It is beautiful because it is full of beauty just as it is, without the need to prove anything or earn anything.

Remember the times when you have felt the safest and the most loved. I'm sure you're thinking of those—family or friends—who were able to welcome and love every little bit of you. They saw your weaknesses and limitations and embraced them as they embraced you.

Consider all the ways the world praises that which it sees as useful within you but shames you for your limitations. It splits you in two. There are the parts of you that can be presented as useful, and parts of you that are hidden because of their perceived uselessness. We hide our vulnerabilities, weaknesses, and limitations because we are inundated with the message that if the useless parts of ourselves were exposed, then *we* would be exposed as useless.

Affirming your whole self as full of beauty and deserving of love and justice is a courageous effort in a world that suppresses us in this way.

This method of dehumanization is not a bug within our current structure of society, but a *feature* of it, and a necessary tool to keep it functioning. A society that is dependent on the labor of its workers benefits when it reduces us to the labor we give to this system of endless production for endless profit.

And so, any religion worth practicing in this society must be one that empowers us to struggle against the systems that dehumanize and devalue us. It may be difficult for some of us to imagine a religion that can empower us in this way, especially because so many of us have experiences in religious communities that increased our dehumanization. And yet, at its core, religion has always been capable of helping people discover their true value. We encounter this alternative method of valuing everything and everyone through the concept of holiness.

HOLY SHIFT

At the core of religious life is the *holy*.

Even though we often associate holiness with moral goodness, that's not the original intent of the concept in the history of religious development, so forget everything you've been taught about what holiness means for a moment. In the Hebrew Bible, the word that gets translated to "holy" is *qadosh*, which literally means "set apart."

Setting something apart as holy was always a way of helping people discover the true nature of things, not to transform their nature. We are the ones who transform when we recognize the holiness of something.

Take the Sabbath, for example. The Sabbath is the culmination of the workweek where we take a day to rest and remind ourselves of our inherent value before we return to our labor where our value is determined by the work we do.

In the biblical narrative, God introduces the Sabbath to the ancient Israelites after they are freed from slavery in Egypt. Imagine the contrast between grueling daily work as enslaved people and a day of rest for the first time as free people. On that day of rest, they are reminded of their true value in contrast to the value assigned to them by their old Egyptian slave masters.

Holy days are days we set apart to spend time away from typical daily activities and reconnect with the self underneath everything we do. Holiness reveals the distinction between our inherent value and the value assigned to us by others.

Creating rituals to help a community remember this truth is a significant function of religion. No matter what society says about us, holiness says something different. Abraham Joshua Heschel explains it beautifully in his essential book *The Sabbath*:

> Six days a week we wrestle with the world, wringing profit from the earth; on the Sabbath we especially care for the seed of eternity planted in the soul. The world has our hands, but our soul belongs to Someone Else.[2]

The assertion that our soul belongs to *Someone Else* is the foundation for resisting any system that attempts to define us for us. My soul does not belong to this capitalist system of endless production and profit. My soul belongs to Someone Else. You cannot reduce me to my usefulness and claim this reduction is me. I am so much more. And whenever I am able to rest from my work, I am reminded of where my value really comes from. I am reminded that I am full of beauty and deserving of love and justice exactly as I am.

FAVORING THE UNFAVORABLE

This theme is clear in the New Testament as well. From the beginning, we can see this in the story of *The Annunciation of Mary*, the mother of Jesus. In the first chapter of the Gospel of Luke we read about a virgin named Mary engaged to a man named Joseph in a little town called Nazareth in Galilee.

Mary is visited by an angel named Gabriel who says, "Greetings, favored one! The Lord is with you."[3]

A visit from an angel is obviously a strange experience—even in the Bible—but the strangest part for Mary is the words the angel chose. The next verse says: "But she was much perplexed by his words and pondered what sort of greeting this might be."

Perhaps Mary is perplexed when an angel calls her favored because she was not in any sort of special position of wealth, or power, or prestige. She is caught off guard when she's called favored because she was *not* favored by the society around her.

The second-century Roman historian Celsus criticized the early Christian movement and considered the story of Jesus's miraculous birth to be absurd. He accused Jesus of making the story up, and Celsus further spread the rumor that Jesus was the illegitimate child "of a poor woman of the country . . . convicted of adultery."[4]

To be clear, Celsus didn't think Jesus's birth story was absurd because he was skeptical of these kinds of supernatural events. There were plenty of stories of miraculous births, including one told of Augustus Caesar, the Roman Emperor at the time of Jesus's birth. According to legend, his mother, Atia, fell asleep inside a temple, and while she slept, the god Apollo disguised himself as a serpent and had sex with her. Ten months later she gave birth to Augustus.

The reason Celsus found the Christian story of a miraculous birth absurd was because it was about someone as poor and powerless as Jesus, with a mother as poor and powerless as Mary. Celsus believed heroes and rulers get miraculous birth stories, not average, forgettable nobodies like a poor Jew from Nazareth.

So, of course, Mary is perplexed by this angel's greeting.

In response to Mary's reaction, the angel says, "Do not be afraid, Mary, for you have found favor with God."

That's the key distinction that begins to bring clarity to Mary's confusion. Mary is favored, but where does this favor come from? It comes from *Someone Else*. Mary has found favor with God, not because she has done anything particularly useful to deserve it, but because she simply is who she is.

The favor Mary found with God is the favor we all share, even while we are consistently unfavored by the society we live in.

Jesus uses his public ministry to announce this special favor we share, but Jesus recognizes that the ones who need to hear this message the most are the ones who are most consistently unfavored in their everyday lives.

So Jesus says, "Blessed are you who are poor, for yours is the kingdom of God. Blessed are you who are hungry now, for you will be filled. Blessed are you who weep now, for you will laugh."[5]

The poor, hungry, and weeping are the ones who least expected to be blessed because of how society had devalued and dehumanized them. By calling them blessed, Jesus reminds them that their value does not come from their position in society, but from somewhere else—from *Someone Else*. To claim that someone is "blessed" is a way of saying God is on their side. A blessing is an assertion that they are favored, they are holy, and they are full of beauty exactly as they are, despite the ways they are devalued by the world around them.

BOTTOM-UP BLESSINGS

These days, we're used to the word "blessed" being used to refer to those who are already filled and already laughing, not to those who are hungry and weeping. The word is often used to refer to the materialistic advantages mostly experienced by those with privilege and power.

And yet, privilege and power are results of historical exploitation at the expense of the poor and powerless—the ones Jesus called *blessed*. Jesus calls the poor and hungry blessed, and says woe to those who are rich and full, so how did we flip that?

Here's an interesting example of this confusion around blessings: In 2020, the evangelical megachurch pastor Louie Giglio suggested Christians use the term "white blessings" instead of the popular term "white privilege" because of the controversial political baggage associated with it. He explained to his congregation, "We understand the curse that was slavery—white people do—and we say that was bad, but we miss the blessing of slavery: that it actually built up the framework for the world that white people live in and lived in."[6]

He was making an analogy to his interpretation of the crucifixion, saying that Jesus became cursed on the cross so that we may live in the blessings achieved as a result of that curse. So he used that symbolism to give a sloppy explanation of the privileges white people have as a result of the "curse of slavery." He was trying to get his uncomfortable white audience to understand their privileged position in society by talking about it in evangelical language. Instead, it sounded like he meant slavery was God's personal blessing given to white people.

After much backlash, he issued an apology saying he misspoke, but when we look at Christian teaching from a historical perspective, we see that Louie Giglio was expressing what many Christians had been communicating for a very long time: that socioeconomic privileges are a sign of God's blessing.

Louie Giglio was just preaching the Protestant work ethic without realizing it.

When the English Puritans colonized the Americas, they used Christian teaching to justify colonization and exploitation of Black and Indigenous people, as did the Spanish, Portuguese, and French Catholics. The English, however, rooted their interpretation of Christianity in the teachings of Protestant Reformer and theologian John Calvin and his intellectual successors.

The Calvinist doctrine of unconditional election dictated the way the English related to non-Europeans. This doctrine claimed God had chosen specific children and predestined them to turn to Christ and go to heaven. As for everyone else, they were predestined to reject Christ and go to hell. The key to the Calvinist doctrine of election is that the election process is based on God's decisions and has nothing to do with our own decisions. It's unconditional. No matter the choices you make in life, if you're one of the chosen, then you are destined for heaven, and if you're not, then you are destined for hell.

On an individual level, it created a tricky dilemma that required a theological solution. How do you know if you're one of God's chosen?

As these Christians looked for a solution, they determined that wealth and property must be signs of God's election. This led to a new justification of socioeconomic hierarchies. If your work led to great wealth and property, then they interpreted this as a sign of God's blessing, which meant you were one of God's elect. So therefore, poverty and a lack of resources was a sign that you weren't one of the elect. This dynamic led colonizers to see the people in the lands they colonized as the non-elect because of a perceived poverty based on the unwillingness to use their lands' resources in the ways colonizers would.

Since enslaved Black and Indigenous people lacked wealth and property as signs of their salvation, they were told they could attain their salvation through hard work. Hard work became a new sign to help determine who was chosen and who was not, and became the avenue for colonized peoples to attain the salvation their colonizers already had, even though the colonizers' salvation was signified by the wealth and property they *stole*. The idea that work can save your soul is the Protestant work ethic, first named by sociologist Max Weber in 1904, who observed the ways this phenomenon was integral to the development of capitalism.

It's easy for us to view this doctrine of election as destructive because of the ways it justified the elect's exploitation of the non-elect, but the initial intention behind its development was really an attempt to avoid this kind of exploitation. This doctrine developed as a corrective to the way the Catholic Church practiced the doctrine of election at the time.

One of several issues Protestants tried to solve was the existential instability every Christian had about where they stood with God. Catholic priests kept this instability alive by frequently demanding monetary offerings to the church as a way to decrease an individual's severity of punishment in the afterlife.

Early Protestant Christian teachers, such as John Calvin, wanted to liberate Christians from this instability and to give every Christian absolute certainty that they are one of God's chosen, no matter how much they do or don't do, or how much they give or don't give. The Protestant doctrine of unconditional election was supposed to give Christians certainty that they are loved, valued, and blessed by God just as they are, and not for their usefulness to the church. The problem of this doctrine arises when you wonder about everyone else. Our natural inclination would be to assume God hates, devalues, and curses everyone else simply because of who they are, no matter what they do.

This doctrine of election was supposed to assure Christians that they are favored by God in a world that disfavors the poor and powerless. The way it has been used to justify colonization and class inequality would likely have been condemned by Calvin, who was also known for frequently preaching on the Christian duty to care for the poor, and against corrupt business practices that exploited the poor.

I understand the need to give Christians existential security in the face of such great insecurity, but if you preach that only a fraction of people are favored by God, then the practical implications of that worldview will always lead to "the elect" justifying their violence and exploitation of "the non-elect."

The way out of this dilemma is to rediscover the favor of God that we all share, no matter our differences.

As 1 Timothy 4:10 says, "We have our hope set on the living God, who is the Savior of all people, especially of those who believe." This doesn't mean those who believe are valued more than those who don't, or that believers receive a special salvation. This God is the Savior of all people.

Christians are not valued by God more than non-Christians. God is the Savior "especially of those who believe" because Christians are called to cultivate a deep awareness of the value we all equally share, and to announce this good news to the world. That's what you see in the book of Acts. The first Christian evangelists announced God's favor to the world, as it was revealed through Jesus, and invited people to embody that truth in community. They believed all humans were made alive in Christ,[7] that all flesh would see salvation,[8] and that the fullness of God fills all in all.[9] This was understood as a gift for all, not a reward for some.

So when Louie Giglio talked about "white blessings," he was unknowingly reflecting the ways that the institutional church has flipped the concept of blessing upside down.

When Jesus declared God's blessing on people, he asserted that those *without* power, privilege, wealth, and property are *blessed*. He announced that God is on their side. The criterion Jesus used to determine on whom to bestow God's blessings was the direct opposite of the criterion developed through the Protestant work ethic.

While it is easy to perceive those with power and privilege as blessed, Jesus would look to the poor and powerless, and declare them blessed. Then he would turn to those with power and privilege and say, as he does in the rest of that passage from Luke, "But woe to you who are rich, for you have received your consolation.

Woe to you who are full now, for you will be hungry.
Woe to you who are laughing now, for you will mourn
and weep."[10]

A CHURCH THAT COMPROMISES

History is filled with stories of the powerful dehumanizing the powerless. The church was supposed to act
alternatively and resist these dehumanizing systems.
Instead, Christian history is filled with Christian leaders perpetuating this dehumanization by preaching that
those who are marginalized by society are also marginalized by God.

When I quote Heschel saying that our soul belongs
to Someone Else, this may not initially sound that liberating, because so many of us have experiences with
Christian communities that simply reframe that "Someone Else" as simply a bigger and more powerful slave
master, instead of the one who desires our liberation
from all types of bondage.

One of the most common ways we see churches perpetuate our dehumanization today is by continuing
to dehumanize LGBTQ+ people. In 2019, the United
Methodist Church—the second largest Protestant
denomination—voted 438 to 384 to keep their traditional ban on same-sex marriage and other LGBTQ-
inclusive practices. The following year they decided to
split into two denominations over the issue.

As long as churches teach that we are supposed to love others, they will not be able to stop people from loving LGBTQ people, no matter how many disclaimers they put in their message of love.

People are gay. People are trans. It isn't sinful. Sin creates an experience of spiritual bondage, and there is no spiritual bondage in being gay or trans. The spiritual bondage we all need freedom from are from the sins of homophobia and transphobia. When homophobia leads to more death, and affirmation leads to more lives saved, then it is clear which one is sinful. More and more homophobic Christians are beginning to realize this. And it's only natural when you're taught to love and value people more than the world does.

When I was a child, I was taught that a church was "compromising" and "giving in to the evil ways of the world" whenever a church was more inclusive of marginalized people, such as LGBTQ people. Now I realize that churches who continue dehumanizing marginalized people are the ones who are compromising with the world.

I was finally fully open about my affirmation of LGBTQ people after I left the Evangelical Church, but I wish I was more open about it earlier. After I left that church, I went to a local Pride event and hung out with a gay friend who used to be a student in my youth group, and that experience made me feel like an authentic minister more than any moment I had as his actual minister. Moments like this made losing all the relationships and opportunities I had lost more than worth it.

THE MATERIAL CONDITIONS THAT ENABLE US TO LOVE OURSELVES

It's clear how spiritual teachings of being favored by God, or of blessedness, or holiness, or grace, can be used to justify inequality. And yet when we look at the root of these teachings, we discover that they can be used to empower our resistance of inequality because we recognize that we deserve better.

Fighting for our collective liberation begins with believing you are worth fighting for. In order to fight for ourselves, we need to have a mustard seed of faith in the truth that we are more valuable than what society says about us.

This shift in perception can motivate us to fight for our collective liberation, but this shift in perception is not enough on its own to accomplish the world we desire.

We all know we need to love ourselves more. We all know we need to heal and reconcile all the fractured perceptions we have of ourselves. A shift in perception can give us a mustard seed of faith to transform our life conditions that hinder us from loving ourselves, but our problems do not get solved with a simple shift in perception.

It is through fighting against our exploitation that we can open up space to begin to authentically love ourselves, and to relate to ourselves in more healthy ways.

In 1968 in Memphis, Tennessee, 1,300 Black sanitation workers went on strike after the deaths of Echol Cole and Robert Walker due to unsafe working conditions. The workers demanded recognition of their newly formed union, better pay, health insurance, and improved working conditions.

After a police assault of the striking workers, Rev. James Lawson spoke to the workers, saying "For at the heart of racism is the idea that a man is not a man, that a person is not a person. You are human beings. You are men. You deserve dignity."[11]

These sentiments were echoed in the slogan of the strike, "I Am a Man." What began as a strike for a better working conditions became a protest for better social conditions, as workers marched the streets with signs that read in huge, bold red letters "I AM A MAN."

Rev. Lawson persuaded Rev. Dr. Martin Luther King Jr. to go to Memphis and support the strike. Two weeks before his assassination, Dr. King gave a speech to the striking sanitation workers, and said, "You are reminding, not only Memphis, but you are reminding the nation that it is a crime for people to live in this rich nation and receive starvation wages."[12]

Ten days later, King returned to march with the workers amid several threats to his life that would lead to his death in Memphis on April 4, 1968. In response to King's assassination, the strike intensified until its end on April 16 when the workers won a settlement that included union recognition and increased wages.

If we want people to relate to themselves in healthier ways, then we must fight against the exploitation that causes their unhealth. If we want people to love themselves, then we must build new material conditions that enable people to love themselves.

In his book *Pedagogy of the Oppressed*, Paulo Freire talks about restoring the dignity to peasant workers in Brazil through alternative methods of education. He says the workers began by constantly putting themselves down, insulting their own intelligence, underestimating themselves, and assuming the superiority of their teachers.

Freire then observed how their self-deprecation changed as soon as their situation of oppression changed. Eventually one peasant leader said, "They used to say we were unproductive because we were lazy and drunkards. All lies. Now that we are respected as men, we're going to show everyone that we were never drunkards or lazy. We were exploited!"[13]

Discovering that you are more valuable than exploitative systems claim you are makes you dangerous. Religion is capable of empowering people to discover this for themselves, so naturally the exploiters have also used religion as a tool to justify exploitation.

Any religion worth practicing today must be one that embraces an alternative method of valuation to empower our resistance of the systems that devalue us. This resistance includes a struggle against our own religious communities that perpetuate our dehumanization; however, critiquing our faith in the name of our faith is nothing new. In fact, it's a sign of an authentic and living faith. This kind of faith resists our dehumanization wherever we find it because our faith teaches us that we deserve to be treated better than the world can ever treat us.

3

WHITE CHRISTIANITY ALL THE WAY DOWN

Growing up in a majority Mexican city in California, I've encountered several white pastors who marketed their church to Mexicans as a form of outreach. They held church events to celebrate Mexican holidays, they released content in Spanish, they promoted their Spanish church services, and they preached sermons about the Christian duty of being hospitable to the local Hispanic community.

I respect ministers' efforts to embrace cultural diversity, but these churches never addressed one crucial problem: that the particular stream of historic Christian teaching that informed their sermons has roots in a colonial interpretation of Christianity. This reinterpretation of the Christian faith was led by European colonizers to justify the exploitation of colonized lands and its inhabitants.

This colonial Christianity is responsible for the development of white supremacy as we know it today. The whiteness that oversaturates the demographics of many Christian congregations may be addressed, but the whiteness that oversaturates the history of Western Christian teaching is often never addressed.

I am now a part of a more Progressive Christian church that actively seeks to address these issues but even within *this* church a colonial interpretation of Christianity has dominated the denomination's history, and it can be felt to this day.

Religion justifies inequality, and religion also empowers us to resist inequality. To understand how this tension has shaped our world, we need to talk about the history of racism and anti-racism. It is important to talk about how the powerful in society have unevenly categorized humans throughout history and how the powerless have resisted categorization because contained within this dynamic are some of the best examples of Christianity being used to justify injustice and to empower resistance.

I know most people don't like to talk about this history, but if we want to change our current situation we have to talk about what got us here. In order to solve issues of racism, we have to be aware that racism did not appear out of nowhere. If racism was simply a pesky intrusive thought, then the solution would be to stop thinking about racism to make it disappear. That doesn't work. Racism runs deeper than that.

FROM COLONIALISM TO RACISM

Racism is experienced through discriminatory actions that reflect the ideology of white supremacy. White supremacy is the justifying ideology of settler colonialism.

It is a result of settler colonialism that I am sitting here in central California writing this book in English on unceded land that historically belongs to the Chumash people. A long history of violence transpired to create this situation.

Settler colonialism is the ongoing imperialist project of expanding the power of a nation by settling in a new land to exploit it for profit. The original inhabitants of the land are either killed or turned into second-class citizens as the new settlers exploit their land and their labor. This exploitation is justified through ideologies that paint second-class citizens as deserving of their exploitation.

White supremacy isn't what creates racial divisions, but it is the ideology that *justifies* racial divisions. White supremacy makes inequality appear justified. White supremacy keeps people from challenging systemic inequality because we have been indoctrinated over the centuries to believe there is something natural about rich, white, cisgender, heterosexual men having easier access to power and wealth than everyone else.

White supremacy must also be understood as a later development of ideologies that justified settler colonialism. The classification of those with black skin as subservient to those with white skin developed after settler colonies had already been established in Africa and the Americas. The classification of whiteness and blackness evolved from a different form of classification that justified the colonialist mission.

So what was the ideology that justified European expansion before white supremacy, and before the concept of "whiteness" even existed? *Christianity.*

WHITE CHRISTIANS AND BLACK PAGANS

White supremacy is a secularization of the way that Christianity was initially used as a justifying ideology for settler colonialism. The classification of diverse European cultural groups into "white" and diverse non-European cultural groups into "black" is rooted in the initial colonial classification of "Christians" and "pagans," or "heathens," or "infidels." In Europe, non-Christians did not receive the same rights as Christians, so the land of non-Christians could be legally stolen, and non-Christians could be legally enslaved. The classification of all humans into "Christians" and "pagans" is what initially gave legitimacy to the mission of European expansion and colonialism.[1]

Christianity was already used to justify colonialism within Europe as Spain and Portugal stole land from Muslim inhabitants, or as European Christians called them, "Saracens." This justifying force can be seen directly in papal bulls written by Pope Nicholas V to King Alfonso V of Portugal, beginning with *Dum Diversas*, a holy decree blessing the king's efforts in the Atlantic slave trade in Africa. Issued on June 18, 1452, the pope granted the king the power

> to invade, search out, capture, vanquish, and subdue all Saracens and pagans whatsoever, and other enemies of Christ wheresoever placed, and the kingdoms, dukedoms, principalities, dominions, possessions, and all movable and immovable goods whatsoever held and possessed by them and to reduce their persons to perpetual slavery, and to apply and appropriate to himself and his successors the kingdoms, dukedoms, counties, principalities, dominions, possessions, and goods, and to convert them to his and their use and profit.[2]

While this papal bull was written specifically for Portugal's mission of expansion, it had an effect on all European colonization. On October 11, 1492, Christopher Columbus observed the Indigenous inhabitants during his first voyage to the Americas and wrote in his diary: "They should be good servants and intelligent, for I observed that they quickly took in what was said to them, and I believe that they would easily be made Christians, as it appeared to me that they had no religion."[3]

Another papal bull, entitled *Inter Caetera*, was issued on May 4, 1493, from Pope Alexander VI to King Ferdinand and Queen Isabella of Spain, in which the pope personally praises Christopher Columbus and his men for having "discovered certain very remote islands and even mainlands that hitherto had not been discovered by others; wherein dwell very many peoples living in peace."[4]

Let's take a moment to acknowledge the absurdity of what we're reading here. Columbus is praised for discovering these islands, "wherein dwell very many peoples living in peace." These decrees created the foundation for what would later be called the Doctrine of Discovery. They gave God-ordained justification for European expansion by creating a narrative of superiority and painting the Indigenous inhabitants as deserving of their exploitation because of their lack of Christian faith.

Pope Alexander VI continues in *Inter Caetera*:

> Moreover, as your aforesaid envoys are of opinion, these very peoples living in the said islands and countries believe in one God, the Creator in heaven, and seem sufficiently disposed to embrace the Catholic faith and be trained in good morals. And it is hoped that, were they instructed, the name of the Savior,

our Lord Jesus Christ, would easily be introduced into the said countries and islands.[5]

Let's be clear here. The mission was *not* to convert foreign people to Christianity. The mission was always to exploit the land and its inhabitants for profit. Offering Christian salvation to the inhabitants of stolen lands was the justifying narrative that allowed colonizers to get support and funding from European Christian monarchs. This narrative also justified genocide and enslavement as holy acts part of a larger mission of Christian evangelism.

Christianity created the initial justification to "capture, vanquish, and subdue" so-called pagans, but as their victims converted to Christianity en masse, a new justification was necessary. The racial categories of "whiteness" and "blackness" developed out of the logical necessity to create new justifications to continue exploiting the land and its inhabitants for European profit.

British, Dutch, French, and Spanish colonizers sold out their old and diverse cultural identities and exchanged them for the broad label of "white" in a move designed to unite all Western European colonizers by giving them cultural superiority over their "black" enemies.

When we critique "whiteness," we are not claiming that people with lighter skin are evil, or anything like that. We are simply pointing out that the initial purpose of using "whiteness" as a racial category is to justify one culturally diverse group's exploitation of several culturally diverse groups by erasing the cultural identities of both "white" people and "nonwhite" people. The ongoing American assimilation of various cultural groups into the category of "white" after formerly being considered nonwhite (such as Irish, Germans, Jews, and Eastern Europeans) is an example of the ongoing cultural erasure on which white supremacy thrives.

The violent categorization and classification of diverse cultural groups into "white" and "black" was the same method of categorization and classification of diverse cultural groups into "Christians" and "pagans." The labels were switched out of a logical necessity to continue justifying the destruction and exploitation of non-Christians and their land.

FOREIGN PEOPLE FROM FOREIGN LANDS

It's important to understand that the *other-ization* of foreign people groups throughout history is never the initial reason for cross-cultural conflict. Rather, the mission of endless expansion and exploitation of foreign peoples' lands is the initial reason for conflict, and then myths and stereotypes that otherize their enemies are developed to reinterpret conquest and exploitation as morally justifiable.

This otherizing tactic is more ancient than Christianity. Ancient civilizations used this tactic of otherizing foreign people groups and described them as wild and savage. They described them as having nonhuman, creature-like qualities, like giant size and extra appendages. Some told stories about foreign peoples being descendants of humans breeding with animals, or angels, or demons.

Framing foreign peoples from foreign lands as dangerous savages gave people the ability to look past the humanity of their enemies, so they might have the strength and courage to destroy them during conflict. Killing your fellow humans becomes a lot less difficult when you believe that if you don't defeat these dangerous savages, then they will surely give in to their barbaric and violent ways and destroy you and your people.

Ancient nations did not choose to attack because they believed the other nation was filled with dangerous savages. The reverse is true. Nations developed myths about other nations filled with dangerous savages to justify war and expansion.

We even see this in the Hebrew Bible. Giants are first mentioned as descendants of fallen angels. Giants appear again when the Israelites scout out the land of Canaan before they seize it. The Israelites claimed that God had promised them the land and was displacing its inhabitants because of their "wickedness." Israelite spies reported that Canaan was filled with giants that would devour them. The giants are occasionally

referenced later during Israel's battles with Canaanites and Philistines, which leads to the famous story
of David facing off against the Philistine giant Goliath
from Gath. Gath was mentioned in the book of Joshua
as a land where some giants remained after the Israelites
wiped out the Canaanites and destroyed their towns.
The final mention of giants is during King David's final
battles with the Philistines in which David and his servants defeat the final giant who had "taunted Israel" and
had "six fingers on each hand, and six toes on each foot,
twenty-four in number."[6]

When we recognize this tactic of justifying conquest
throughout history by otherizing foreign peoples, it is
difficult to ignore. This tactic is not just in the Bible,
but in many other ancient texts and art as well. We
also see it at the birth of Western civilization in Greek
mythology, art, and literature. From Herakles to Odysseus, the Greeks told stories of warrior heroes battling
savage creatures in foreign lands filled with unused
resources.[7]

Before defeating the one-eyed monster called a Cyclops,
Odysseus makes note of the "unsown and untilled" fer-
tile island of the Cyclopes. These stories didn't make
people think that peoples of distant lands were savage
creatures. These stories were projections of what people
already believed about people living on distant lands and
provided convenient descriptors of foreign peoples that
justified conquest. Greek geographer Strabo described
the Albanians as "living a Cyclopean life" when explaining

their inability to use their land and sea "to the full extent of its value."[8]

SAVING SAVAGE SOULS

This tactic of justifying conquest goes back much further than Christianity, but the particular type of otherizing we find ourselves in is a result of Christianity being used as a justifying ideology, and Christians must be honest about that today. The ideological mission of saving the souls of savages runs deeper than we realize, even among those who imagine themselves free from any sort of Christian worldview. We all still classify others based on the paradigm of "civilizing immoral and primitive savages through Christian salvation," but with different language and categories.

We can see it in modern descriptions of religion, ranging from more progressive forms of spirituality to modern atheism. The way we talk about religion in general is still often rooted in the way Christian colonizers described Indigenous religions: as simply a form of irrational superstitious fetishism.

The word "fetishism" was used in the anthropology of religion centuries before it was used to describe sexual fetishes. The word is a translation of the Portuguese word *feitico*, which comes from the Latin *factitius*, meaning "artificial." The Portuguese colonizers of the fifteenth century used the word to refer to the use of sacred objects by subjected West Africans during their rituals of worship. The colonizers viewed the "fetishi-zation" of these objects as a sign of an inferior and prim-itive religion, centered around an irrational belief that material objects contained supernatural power.[9]

So the colonial descriptions and classifications of Indigenous spirituality were trusted throughout Europe and used by anthropologists with little pushback until centuries later.

I imagine fifteenth-century West Africans would have described their use of sacred objects quite dif-ferently than their colonizers did, especially because this interpretation of African spirituality as irrational fetishism was intentionally developed to justify the exploitation of African people.

In the eighteenth century, many Enlightenment phi-losophers adopted this view of Indigenous religions, and in the spirit of progress and modernity they devel-oped the idea that the irrational superstitions of Indige-nous religions represented a primitive form of religion, while Christianity represented a more evolved form of religion. One of the earliest versions of this theory was published in 1760 by writer Charles de Brosses, who used the concept of fetishism in African religions to explain ancient Greek polytheism. His theory was that all religions begin in this primitive stage that Africans still happen to be in.

The concept of maturing and evolving stages of faith and spirituality is a popular one, used in many differ-ent contexts today with various descriptions of what these stages of growth should look like. Many popular spiritual teachers speak of religion this way and depict a more open-minded faith with limited doctrines and definitions as the latest and most desirable stage of an evolving spirituality. While this concept of evolving stages within spirituality has helped many people escape toxic and abusive religious environments, we must also recognize its roots when we observe that the first "level" or "stage" is often represented by Indigenous religions participating in a "primitive" form of religion. The origin of that classification is Christian colonizers reductively redefining the rituals of Indigenous cultures to justify the destruction of their cultures.

Modern atheists took this Enlightenment explanation of religion and determined that *all* forms of religion should be classified as primitive supernatural fetishism, including Christianity. Instead of challenging Christians' reductive description of Indigenous religions, they decided it was an accurate description and claimed that Christianity fit that reductive description as well, along with every other religion. This reductive theory of religion is clearly seen in the work of the New Atheist movement, which gained popularity after the increase in Islamophobia after the September 11 attacks, but we also see it in the work of old influential atheists such as Ludwig Feuerbach, Karl Marx, and Sigmund Freud. They adopted a European colonial interpretation of religion without fully comprehending the source of it.

Christian colonizers defined Indigenous religions as backward, irrational, and superstitious as part of their larger tactic of justifying the enslavement and genocide of Indigenous peoples. Atheists who adopt this theory of religion run the risk of perpetuating the dehumanization of others who do not meet their expectations of "rational thinking." You are not free from this destructive ideology just because you add Christianity to the list of primitive religions.

The European Christian colonial classification of humans is the ideology we are *all* swimming in. It is so pervasive that it will adapt to any group identity, even among the atheists who may have thought they were safe by being characteristically anti-Christian. No one is safe. This is the worldview we are all born into if your country was colonized by Christians. The labels and the categories may change, but it is still the same old story of the civilized saving the world from the savages.

Progressivism is one of the latest developments of this justifying ideology for settler colonialism. Originating in the early twentieth century with causes such as modernizing towns by destroying Indigenous landmarks, displacing people of color from their cities through gentrification, popularizing eugenics before Nazi Germany, and violently intervening in foreign affairs, Progressives were committed to making the world more civilized and rational by removing anything that made society look uncivilized and irrational.

The "progress" in the name "Progressive" was a reference to progressing away from the "barbarism" of "uncivilized" peoples. Although the values and policy positions of early twenty-first-century Progressives are obviously very different from those of Progressives one hundred years earlier, both twentieth- and twenty-first-century Progressives often share a similar motivation. After all, twenty-first-century Progressives often assert that injustices such as racism, sexism, ableism, homophobia, transphobia, environmental harm, and wealth inequality are all unfavorable because they are representative of the values of a more primitive and irrational society, and that these injustices must be overcome in order to achieve a more civilized and enlightened society.

During Donald Trump's presidency, the common insults that many Progressives had for Trump's supporters usually included an overwhelming amount of ableism and classism. The only explanation many could come up with for someone supporting Trump was that they must be uncivilized and irrational. For four years they found every way imaginable to call Trump supporters "dumb" and "poor," revealing a disdain for the "uncivilized." Hillary Clinton calling Trump's supporters "deplorables" is an easy example of this tendency.

Progressive Christians in the twentieth and twenty-first centuries have tended to follow suit. Many Progressives and Progressive Christians truly do care about liberation and decolonization, but they have a duty to dissect and exorcise the ways Christian colonialism has infected the foundation of their worldview.

Dig deep into the foundational ideologies that support the nations that have settled North and South America. You will discover that it is nothing but white Christianity all the way down. And what has grown out of those foundations is every form of social division that we are actively fighting today.

A HOLY BLASPHEMY

It should come as no surprise that many people who have been historically abused in the name of Christianity now want nothing to do with Christianity.

Some of us want to reclaim the radical elements at the root of the Christian faith and use them as tools to empower our resistance of institutions that maintain injustice. That's a major part of what this book is about. However, others have been so abused by the Christian church that they have no desire to reclaim it. In these cases, it seems like the path to liberation for these individuals requires an absolute rejection of the entire Christian faith. Throughout Christian history we see examples of people who needed to reject Christianity to find liberation, especially when we look at the lives of those who have been victims of Christian violence.

In his essay "Voices from a Living Hell," Javier Villa-Flores talks about a common pattern of a special kind of blasphemy from enslaved people in Spanish-controlled

Latin America in the sixteenth and seventeenth cen-turies.[10] Some enslaved people realized they could take advantage of the Spanish Inquisition's court system, which required slaveholders to bring them to trial if they were caught blaspheming God. Some enslaved people took this opportunity, while they were being brutally beaten, to renounce God and the saints to stop the beating. This worked especially if there were public witnesses.

This put the slaveholder at a disadvantage. In order to take their enslaved worker to court, the owner had to pay for travel, pay for the potentially lengthy stay in prison, and lose the enslaved worker's labor power during the duration of this process. The slaveholder also risked being ordered to sell their enslaved worker for a decreased market value, since unruly slaves who had been tried by the Holy Office were difficult to resell.

In court, the enslaved person placed the blame on their enslavers for forcing them to blaspheme and thus "lose their soul," by creating excessively cruel work-ing conditions through brutal abuse and chastisement. Sometimes this strategy was successful and the enslaved person was transferred to a new enslaver.

Sometimes blasphemy can be used as a tool to expose the Christian authorities that have made your life a liv-ing hell.

After all, which is more blasphemous to the God who frees enslaved people in the Bible: the enslaver who beats an enslaved person in the name of God, or the enslaved person who verbally blasphemes God to stop the beating?

Throughout history, victims of Christian violence have blasphemed God for more honest reasons than tricking the court of the Inquisition. And they had every reason to do so.

Direct blasphemy by the exploited exposes the indirect blasphemy of their exploiters. When people look back at these moments in history, it is clear that the blasphemy of the exploited is justified because of their suffering.

When we read stories like this, it is easy to admit that specific individuals are justified in rejecting the Christian faith, but we must also admit that the path to liberation required them to reject the Christian faith when the only Christian faith available was one that exploited and abused them. Much of the violence committed over the last two thousand years has been in the name of Christianity, and so naturally many people have rejected the Christian faith as a way of gaining freedom from some of the Christian violence that is still committed to this day.

A significant example of ongoing Christian violence is the violence committed against transgender people today, fueled by anti-trans Christian rhetoric. I have trans friends who I know have rejected Christianity and can never return because of the traumatic memories of spiritual, psychological, and physical abuse they faced from their family and church. I also have trans friends who have reclaimed their Christian faith through liberative trans-affirming expressions of Christianity, but we shouldn't expect everyone to do that work, especially while Christianity is still actively used to justify violence against them.

It's important that Christians be honest about this history, not so that we may be overcome with sorrow and shame, but so that we can understand the healing and reparation that we are called to take part in. A knowledge of historic Christian violence does not have to be debilitating for Christians. It can be liberating.

The good news is that Christian violence does not live in our hearts. If it did, then it would be difficult to determine a tangible solution. Rather, Christian violence lives in our institutions that perpetuate our exploitation. And it is by confronting the origin of these institutions that we can envision their end.

Christian colonizers do not have the final word on our destiny. By unveiling the significant points in history when colonizers reinterpreted the Christian faith, we can affirm that what has been constructed can be deconstructed. What has been established can be dismantled. What has been institutionalized can be abolished. What has been colonized can be decolonized.

Christians must choose between a faith that continues to justify colonization and a faith that empowers decolonization. Colonization has shaped our history. Decolonization will shape our future.

4

TAKING AND RESHAPING JESUS

I first encountered critiques of historic Christian violence in books and talks by Progressive Christians. Christian colonialism was often framed within a larger message about our need to repent for the ways we've colonized and marginalized people. This inspired me because I came from an environment where Christians never took responsibility for historic Christian violence.

Then I began studying the history of colonialism from a secular perspective, and I realized something that I had missed for years. All those books I was reading were by *white* Progressive Christians speaking to other white Progressive Christians, with no sense of narrowness whenever they used the word "we."

As a Mexican American, my people are some of the people who have been colonized and marginalized through Christian violence. I was hindered from realizing the ways my family and my people were victims of Christian colonialism.

Obviously, there are ways that we all still perpetuate colonial Christianity and white supremacy, simply because those ideologies are so ingrained in all of us that we justify them unintentionally, if not intentionally. It's important that we all take responsibility for that. But by only engaging with the history of colonialism from the perspective of the descendants of colonizers, I was ignorant of my own people's experience of violent suppression and cultural erasure. Having a space to collectively repent isn't enough. I need a space to heal. And I need a space to begin reshaping my faith free from white supremacy.

It's a common experience for people of color to realize they've been seeing themselves through a white lens. It's difficult to name our own experience when we are constantly indoctrinated with others' descriptions of our experience and pressured to affirm their descriptions in order to survive.

When we can name our own experience in our own way, we will be empowered to build a new world that intentionally serves all of us everywhere.

I'm inspired and empowered by all those who have reshaped the Christian faith for the sake of the work of liberation. When we can be honest about the violence in the history of Christianity, then we can also understand how profound it is that some people have reclaimed their Christian faith while fighting against the unjust systems that Christianity has been used to justify.

I am not talking about a naive surrender to an oppressive religion. Those who are empowered by their Christian faith to fight against injustice also critically reject Christianity whenever it takes an oppressive form.

Slavery abolitionist leader Frederick Douglass was empowered by his Christian faith to escape slavery and commit to the abolition of slavery, while simultaneously rejecting the Christianity that sought to justify his enslavement. In the appendix of his first autobiography in 1845, he wrote:

> What I have said respecting and against religion, I mean strictly to apply to the slaveholding religion of this land, and with no possible reference to Christianity proper; for, between the Christianity of this land, and the Christianity of Christ, I recognize the widest possible difference—so wide, that to receive the one as good, pure, and holy, is of necessity to reject the other as bad, corrupt, and wicked.[1]

Douglass also saw himself aligned with anyone who rejected "the slaveholding religion of this land," even if they did not embrace the Christianity of Christ he fought for. In an 1852 speech entitled "What to the Slave Is the Fourth of July?" he says, "Welcome infidelity! Welcome atheism! Welcome anything! In preference to the gospel, as preached by those Divines!"[2]

Douglass did not distinguish between the Christianity of this land and the Christianity of Christ in order to say that those who follow slaveholder religion are just fake Christians, or to claim that if they were to follow the Christianity of Christ like Douglass, then they would be real Christians. We have a tendency to make that generalization when we talk about Christian violence.

When other people expose Christian violence, we may get defensive and say, "Well those violent people aren't real Christians," and then go on to talk about fringe groups of real Christians fighting injustice that most people have never heard of. The fact that these "real Christians" are so marginal exposes the absurdity of claiming that the louder, more powerful, wealthier, and more influential Christians aren't real Christians.

Douglass wasn't playing that game. He was making the opposite point, which is why he refers to slaveholding religion as "the religion of this land." He goes on to clarify: "I mean by the religion of this land, that which is revealed in the words, deeds, and actions of those bodies, north and south, calling themselves Christian churches, and yet in union with slaveholders."[3]

The violence revealed in the words, deeds, and actions of the organizations that call themselves Christian churches all over the land is as real as you can imagine. Oppressive versions of Christianity wield the most power and influence, so claiming those Christians aren't real Christians is a dangerously inappropriate response to people who address Christianity's history of violence.

Embracing a Christian faith of resistance of injustice requires a resistance of dominant Christian powers and ideologies that justify injustice. I'm inspired by stories of colonized and marginalized people taking the Christian faith to its radical conclusions and being empowered by their faith to fight for collective liberation.

Take, for example, the story of the Virgin of Guadalupe. The Spanish Catholic colonizers gave to Indigenous people the image of a beautiful, pale-skinned Virgin Mary who had, according to legend, appeared to Juan Diego in Mexico City in 1531, and could be prayed to for miracles. It's likely that the church created this story themselves, and if not, then they still shaped its retelling in order to give Indigenous communities a feminine symbol to replace their goddesses.

But, over time, Mexicans used the symbol of the Virgin of Guadalupe to empower their resistance. The Mexican War of Independence from Spain in 1810 began with the Catholic priest Miguel Hidalgo crying out, "Death to the Spaniards and long live the Virgin of Guadalupe!" Mexican depictions of the Virgin were also created with darker and darker skin over the centuries. Mexican soldiers fought against the Spanish in 1810 and in the Mexican Revolution in 1910, carrying flags depicting a darker skinned Virgin Mary who looked more like the Mexicans and less like the Spanish who gave them the image centuries earlier.

They did not take an inherently oppressive symbol and transform it to a liberative one. They took a symbol that was used to oppress them, and then through their own engagement with Christian symbolism they discovered its original liberative characteristics that were missed by their oppressors. They were reclaiming the Virgin Mary of the Bible who praised the Lord for bringing down the powerful from their thrones and sending the rich away empty.[4]

For Mexicans, the Virgin of Guadalupe is a symbol of power that serves as a reminder of the power used against us and the power we have within us to overcome.

Using Christianity to colonize usually backfires eventually because colonized peoples end up discovering that the God they were forced to worship is really on their side. They discover that the God of the Bible is a God who frees enslaved people and condemns those who exploit them. The colonized discover that the Christian story is a story of a God saving people like them from the type of people that forced Christianity on them.

MAKING JESUS OURS

I'm reminded of the story in Matthew 15 of a Canaanite woman who runs to Jesus and shouts, "Have mercy on me, Lord, Son of David; my daughter is tormented by a demon."

> But he did not answer her at all. And his disciples came and urged him, saying, "Send her away, for she keeps shouting after us." He answered, "I was sent only to the lost sheep of the house of Israel." But she came and knelt before him, saying, "Lord, help me." He answered, "It is not fair to take the children's food and throw it to the dogs." She said, "Yes, Lord, yet even the dogs eat the crumbs that fall from their masters' table." Then Jesus answered her, "Woman, great is your faith! Let it be done for you as you wish." And her daughter was healed instantly.[5]

Jesus was solely concerned with preaching his message to his fellow Jews. "Dogs" was a common insult Jews gave to gentiles (non-Jews). Jesus reminds this woman that his message is for the children of Israel, like *him*, and not dogs, like *her*. Instead of accepting Jesus's rejection, the woman challenges Jesus to change his mind. She cleverly shoots back, "even the dogs eat the crumbs that fall from the master's table." Jesus is transformed by this, which shouldn't shock us because Jesus was human, so of course he was capable of learning and expanding—he was teachable.

This woman challenged Jesus's mission and stretched it wider for the sake of those whom Jesus hadn't yet addressed. When the liberation Jesus offered wasn't made available for her, she had to take it. And Jesus commends the woman's faith.

In 1971, on the television program *Soul!,* Nikki Giovanni and James Baldwin, two Black poets and Civil Rights activists, had a dialogue about the problems faced by their two generations in fighting for racial equality.[6] At one point they discussed their contentious relationship with the church, as Nikki Giovanni said she "digs the church" but "can't dig the theology." She then shared a story about realizing how much she was still deeply influenced by the Baptist Church she grew up in. "I went up to an A.M.E. Zion Church and a lady was singing 'Yes, Jesus Loves Me' and people started shouting. People were shouting. And it hit me as I was sitting there—my God, as a so-called Black militant I have nothing stronger to offer than Jesus. It blew my mind."

James Baldwin laughed with Giovanni as she shared this revelation, and then abruptly got serious for a moment, and said, "Baby, what we did with Jesus was not supposed to happen. We took him. We took that cat over and made him ours. He has nothing whatever to do with that white Jesus in Montgomery, Alabama, in that white church. We did something else with him. We made him ours."

Taking Jesus and reshaping him to empower the work of liberation is an important calling. And this calling has been embodied throughout Christian history, from the Canaanite woman to civil rights activists. This work may seem like a manipulation of an ancient message to the critics, but it is often motivated by the desire to uncover the radical roots of the message that are ignored by the popular teaching of the time.

REINTEGRATING WHAT WAS STOLEN FROM US

This process of taking and reshaping ideologies comes naturally to colonized peoples and their descendants because most of the cultural resources we work with were never ours to begin with. And most of the cultural resources that originally belonged to us were suppressed or destroyed by Christian colonizers.

As a Mexican, I share ancestry with both Spanish and Indigenous people, but can never fully belong to either cultural identity because of that historical mixture. My people exist in a liminal space between both cultures, and the disorientation of this liminality is exacerbated by my identity as a Mexican American under the dominating pressure of American culture. Working with a hybrid of philosophical and spiritual ideas is natural to me because hybridity defines my cultural existence in this liminal space in between various cultures.

This hybridity makes some people uncomfortable, but I'm used to it. White Christians often tell me that I can't be politically leftist while being a Christian, and white leftists often tell me that I can't be a Christian while being politically leftist. Both of those perspectives perpetuate the European colonial interpretation of Christianity, which says that one must only be the type of Christian that promotes the colonial mission. That interpretation of Christianity was designed to destroy the cultural identity and resources of colonized peoples.

To submit and comply with the demands of white Christians or white leftists who would like me to reject a part of my identity would be to further divide myself in a world that actively divides me and isolates me from the cultural resources I need to survive. I reclaim my dignity and shamelessly embrace my full identity by allowing myself to exist in a state of multiplicity despite the pressure to conform to any singular identity.

In a similar way I also reject the demands of Christians who wish I was more doctrinally aligned with popular Christian orthodoxy, or so-called correct Christian teaching. I have no interest in aligning with the religious convictions of a special branch of European Christians, no matter which special branch of European Christians you think is the right one. I know many Mexican Christians and other Christians of color who value theological orthodoxy more than I do, but the frequent demand that I become more orthodox comes almost exclusively from white Christians.

Reshaping our faith looks like widening our faith beyond the boundaries of so-called correct Christian teaching. Christian denominations and academies do not get to decide the best way to express our faith. Their motivation is preservation. The motivation behind colonized Christians reshaping our faith is liberation.

A major reason Black and Indigenous people could embrace Christianity was because their original spiritual resources had been stolen from them. Indigenous spirituality from pre-colonial Africa and the Americas was demonized and suppressed as part of the mission of settler colonialism. So one of the ways we reshape our faith today is by reintegrating some of those cultural and spiritual resources that were demonized.

It's been inspiring for me to see Black, Indigenous, and Latinx Christians integrate Indigenous spiritual rituals and teaching into their Christian faith. One of the ways this reintegration is expressed is through rediscovering our spiritual connection with our ancestors. In American and African Indigenous spirituality, the ancestors are still with us, experiencing the world at the same time we are, and guiding us to become whom we are called to be. Christian colonizers claimed our ancestors were in hell. They were wrong. They demonized our ancestors to convince us that we needed to be saved from our culture. Reconnecting with our ancestors means refusing to demonize them and recognizing their ancient wisdom as significant for living out our faith today.

This reintegration also looks like rediscovering the spiritual significance of nature and widening our faith to encounter God within nature. Nature is no longer profane, but sacred, just as our Indigenous ancestors always understood.

This reintegration also looks like reconnecting to the material dimension of worship through sacred objects like candles, prayer cards, photographs, and statues, along with shrines in which to place all our sacred objects. Worship with sacred objects was suppressed by Christian colonizers, who claimed this form of worship was irrational, and now colonized Christians are reintegrating the use of sacred objects into their religious life with a fresh appreciation, recognizing the value that comes from infusing objects with shared spiritual meaning.

Colonized Christians reintegrating the cultural resources of Indigenous spirituality is one of the ways we empower ourselves so that we may liberate ourselves from settler colonialism. This reintegration should be a priority in order to develop a liberative Christian faith that empowers us to decolonize.

My friend Bryan started a group within his church strictly for BIPOC (Black, Indigenous, and People of Color) to support one another in personal and collective healing. These BIPOC-only groups are essential. Progressive churches preaching against racism and embodying a spirit of repentance is not enough. Providing a space for repentance may be fulfilling for white Christians, but Christians of color need our own space for healing. We also need spaces like this in which to support one another as we reshape our faith on our own terms.

I BELIEVE IN THE GOD OF THE OPPRESSED

I have rejected the Christianity I grew up with, which is the religion of this land. As a way of discovering my own dignity, I reject the Christianity that has been responsible for so much oppression. However, I am also empowered to discover my own dignity *because* of my Christian faith. But my faith is not the Christian faith of the colonizers. It's the Christian faith of colonized and marginalized peoples throughout history who were able to discover that this God is really on our side, empowering us to fight oppression.

There is historic Christian teaching that was developed to justify colonization, and there is historic Christian teaching that was developed by colonized peoples to empower their struggle for freedom. Contemporary Christian teaching is a result of many centuries of both types of Christian teaching melded together. Contemporary Christians have a responsibility to sift through those historic Christian teachings to discover which kind of God they affirm as a Christian today.

I believe in the God of the oppressed, and I reject the God of the oppressors. In order to live out an authentic Christian faith, I have to wrestle with both of these conceptions of God because both of them are claimed by Christians. I am inspired and empowered by various liberative Christian teachings from colonized and marginalized peoples, such as Latin American liberation theology, interpreting the Christian faith from the perspective of the poor and oppressed in Latin America, as well as Black liberation theology, from the perspective of Black people; womanist theology, from the perspective of Black women; mujerista theology, from the perspective of Latina women; queer theology, from the perspective of LGBTQ people; and other liberative theologies that have developed as distinct methods of interpretation over the last century. These various intersectional and liberative Christian expressions are the reason Christianity is still meaningful to me today.

Over the last couple of decades, many white Progressive Christians have become successful authors and influencers, having been propped up as the leaders of a new Christian reformation. However, most of their success is due to their ability to popularize these liberative Christian expressions for white liberal audiences. If we are in the middle of a historic Christian reformation, it is because of the liberative theologies developed by colonized and marginalized Christians over the last century, not because of the white theologians who profit off them.

GOOD IDEAS AREN'T GOOD ENOUGH

When I discuss liberation theology in activist spaces, I'll often hear non-Christians say things like, "I don't like

Christianity, but liberation theology is cool." Those of us who have actively pursued more liberative expressions of Christianity hear statements like this all the time because these liberative expressions, while inspiring and life-giving, are marginal in the face of "the Christianity of this land."

Obviously, we would like our perspective to be the norm among Christians, instead of the oppressive forms of Christianity that justify colonization, but first, we must recognize why oppressive forms of Christianity are so popular.

The Christianity of this land is a result of Christianity having been used to justify the mission of settler colonialism. Oppressive Christian teachings did not inspire settler colonialism. Rather, people gradually developed oppressive Christian teachings to interpret settler colonialism as morally justifiable. This Christian ideology evolved into the white supremacist ideologies we are more familiar with today.

The order is really important here. Oppression *precedes* the ideology that justifies oppression, so Christian teachings that justify oppressive institutions will remain the norm as long as these oppressive institutions exist. Christian teachings that empower our fight for liberation can only have space to become the norm *after* the abolition of these oppressive institutions.

We can travel all over, sharing alternative Christian teachings and converting people one by one, but it will never be at a rate effective enough to abolish oppressive institutions. It is through the abolition of oppressive institutions that people can have space to begin to truly believe in a God who empowers the oppressed to struggle for freedom.

Before the abolition of slavery in the United States, the majority of American Christians believed God condoned slavery. That didn't change until after the abolition of slavery. Abolitionist Christians existed, and there were denominational splits over the issue, but the abolition of slavery wasn't made possible through those abolitionist Christians persuading their fellow Christians to change their minds. Their fellow Christians were only able to gain space to change their minds once slavery was abolished. Before it was abolished, many Christians didn't have the ability to imagine God beyond a God that ordained the status quo. The same lack of imagination exists today.

This is how most beliefs function. We rationalize and internalize the reality that has been institutionalized in our everyday lives. We naturally want to assume that there must be a good reason that things are the way they are, and that people much smarter than us must have set things up this way. Obviously, individuals can change their minds on their own, but the only way to change minds on a mass scale is to transform the institutions in our everyday lives to give people a new reality to rationalize and internalize. This is how minds change en masse, for better or for worse.

Before a massive transformation, people fight and cling to their old conceptions of God, claiming that those who are trying to transform things are working against God, who carefully set things up the way they are. Then, after the transformation takes place, people praise God for leading the way for this necessary historic change.

So when the enslaved Christian preacher Nat Turner discovered that God is on the side of the oppressed, he knew that this revelation could only be understood by the people of the United States through the abolition of slavery, not through simply teaching people that God desires the abolition of slavery. Nat Turner was known for being an exceptionally gifted communicator, but he used those skills to organize his fellow enslaved people and lead a violent rebellion against their enslavers in 1831.

Nat Turner grew up in what was supposed to be the good, liberal, Christian alternative of a slave plantation. He did not experience particularly harsh treatment or abuse, compared to enslaved people on other plantations. He learned to read and was taught the Bible from an early age. What the slaveholders who maintained these more "civilized" plantations didn't understand was that there was no possible version of slavery that could ever be tolerable for enslaved people. Nat Turner exposed that.

In *A Theological Account of Nat Turner*, Karl Lampley describes the significance of Nat Turner's slave rebellion in the historical fight to end slavery:

It signaled the death of slavery in America. Turner's insurrection meant that slavery and Christianity were fundamentally incompatible. No longer could Christian slave-masters hide behind religious and theological justifications of cruelty and brutality. Turner's revolt indicated that blacks could not be enslaved indefinitely. The impulse to rebellion and liberation had invaded the consciousness of black slave religion. Turner's prophetic violence pronounced condemnation and judgment on the institution of slavery. From thereafter, slave rebellion became a reality and concrete fear of white Virginians culminating finally in the Civil War and emancipation.[7]

To affirm Nat Turner's Christian faith requires a different conceptualization of the Christian faith than the popular options we have available to us today. The faith of Nat Turner is a stumbling block to the versions of Christianity that exist as a justifying force for oppressive institutions. Affirming Nat Turner as a good Christian who justly followed God short-circuits our typical Christian worldview and creates an opening for an alternative religious expression.

ANOTHER WAY

People are getting fed up with religion because people are getting fed up with the status quo. Being fed up with the status quo means being simultaneously fed up with the ideologies and practices that justify the status quo. People are fed up with religion for the same reason they're fed up with nationalism, patriarchy, white supremacy, and cis heteronormativity. With the desire to change the current state of things comes the desire to let go of the ideologies that justify the current state of things. For many people, that is all religion seems to be good for.

However, there is another type of religious expression. It begins with affirming the inherent and unconditional dignity shared by all of us, and then it leads to resistance of the systems that categorize humans above other humans. This type of religious expression resists the oppressive systems that devalue us, even if that means resisting a popular version of our religion. This was the religion of Nat Turner. As Lampley notes, "Turner recognized the glaring inconsistency between his personal attributes and worth before God and his actual place in front of white society."[8]

This type of religious expression is why Jesus is still so important to me. Jesus was surrounded by fellow teachers whose religion was used to justify the social divisions present in the Roman Empire of the first century. Jesus's religion empowered him to challenge the social divisions of his day, and so he intentionally blessed those who were the most devalued and dehumanized by society. Religious authorities condemned Jesus for whom he chose to associate with. Jesus condemned those who used their religion to justify their discrimination.

Each of us are many things. We aren't just oppressed or oppressor. Employer or employee. Rich or poor. Black, or white, or brown. Each of us are so much more than that, and we each deserve the freedom to explore the entirety of our vast and unique identities. We can resist the ways we are reduced to a few identity markers by treating one another with respect, but no matter how we treat one another, there are still unavoidable systemic barriers that perpetuate our division.

The mission of settler colonialism and the Christian teachings that justified it run deep within the structure of the institutions that shape our society, from government, to education, to culture, to health care, to the criminal punishment system. Abolishing the institutions that maintain our inequalities is the only way to open up space for Christian teachings that preach equality to become the norm. Christian history is filled with those who understood this and were empowered by their faith to resist the institutions that used Christianity to oppress them. Those who choose to continue this important work today are joining a long line of Christians who helped shape the path toward our collective liberation.

5

REVELATIONS AND REPARATIONS

I grew up hearing testimonies quite often in church. Someone would get on the stage with a microphone, then tell a story about how they hit rock bottom in life before Jesus saved them. I heard stories about drug addiction, poverty, disease, domestic violence, sexual abuse, abandonment, and all sorts of loss. Then they would talk about how these tragedies led them to make destructive decisions in order to cope, which only made their situation worse. Then, in the midst of all that struggle, they had an experience with Jesus. They discovered that they were deeply loved by Jesus and had a purpose in life.

I used to be jealous of these powerful stories since I was just a church kid and didn't have life experiences as intense as these. My parents did, and so did many of their friends, but I never did. However, these stories enabled me to understand Jesus as someone who loves us at rock bottom and lifts us up.

A common problem in Christian communities that center these testimonies is the stifling behavior management the church enforces after these conversion experiences, which forces people to feel like they can only have a few rock-bottom moments before they no longer deserve grace. However, I always understood Jesus as full of grace and forgiveness at every turn in our lives, no matter what any hypocritical Christians had to say.

This message of grace and forgiveness is what attracts a lot of people to Christianity. Discovering a God that forgives you no matter what you've done or what you've been through can be incredibly transformative.

The nature of forgiveness is always excessive. Forgiveness always goes over and beyond to respond to great sin with greater grace.[1]

WHO DID JESUS FORGIVE?

Jesus commonly forgave people after healing them and taught his disciples to forgive others generously, but contemporary Christians often describe forgiveness very narrowly. We typically understand forgiveness as pardoning someone for the harm they caused. This is an inadequate understanding of forgiveness.

Forgiveness can look like pardoning harm, but that's like defining hospitality as inviting friends to your house party. Hospitality can look like that, but hospitality is clearly so much more than that. And it is out of a spirit of hospitality that you would invite your friends. So out of a spirit of forgiveness, you can pardon someone for harm they caused you, but forgiveness is so much more than that.

If pardoning harm is all Jesus meant by forgiveness, then Jesus would have gone around pardoning those guilty of the greatest harm. Jesus didn't do that. Instead, Jesus went to those who had the greatest amount of harm done *to* them and forgave them.

We must see forgiveness with a wider lens if we want to understand what Jesus was doing.

The Jewish tradition informed the way Jesus and his followers thought about forgiveness. Judaism and early Christianity scholar Bruce Chilton explains that the Jewish conception of forgiveness is best understood as a release from the "incapacitating shackle" of sin.[2]

Sin constrains. Forgiveness releases.

Chilton goes on to say that the "current, weakened conception of forgiveness as merely overlooking or forgetting the harm one has suffered is a far cry from the Judaic sense of liberation from the consequences of one's own deeds."

Using this understanding of forgiveness, philosopher and theologian John Caputo also brilliantly explains, "Forgiveness is not an exercise of power but a forgoing of the exercise of power, giving up the power one has over the other."[3]

It's also important to understand that concepts like sin, forgiveness, and reconciliation were always understood as collective, not individual. Sin refers to the sin of the community, not the person. And the *community* desires forgiveness and reconciliation.

However, the guilt for the sin of the community commonly falls onto those who struggle the most to survive in that community. Throughout history, marginalized people have been scapegoated for society's ills. Like rain gathering at the bottom of a hill, the guilt for the sin of society always rolls down toward the marginalized masses. In the same way that marginalized people today may be described as lazy, ignorant, and selfish, they were described in Jesus's society as sinful, demonic, and spiritually unclean. Jesus befriends them. And he heals them. Then he forgives them, releasing and relieving them from the guilt and pressure of society's sin.

Jesus did not go out of his way to forgive the individuals guilty of the most harm, such as kings and rulers. He went out of his way to forgive individuals who had the most harm done *to* them, such as beggars, enslaved people and lepers. These people were constrained by the sin of society and needed to be liberated from that burden.

The sick and disabled people Jesus healed were marginalized in every way. They were marginalized economically because of their inability to work, which is why many of the people Jesus healed were beggars or enslaved people. They were marginalized spiritually because people with diseases or disabilities were labeled ritually unclean and were prohibited from entering the Jewish temple. And according to temple law, touching someone who was ritually unclean would also make you unclean, so they were socially marginalized as well.

Sometimes Jesus healed people and then commanded them to go show themselves to the priests and to make an offering for their cleansing as a testimony against the priests who excluded them from the temple. Jesus's healings were a direct challenge to the society that marginalized them.

After healing people, Jesus said, "Your sins are forgiven." I'm sure these people committed petty misdeeds every now and then such as stealing, lying, and fighting. These are the misdeeds the poor often commit as they struggle to survive. However, this isn't the shackle of sin they needed freedom from. The economic, spiritual, and social marginalization perpetuated by an unequal society is the shackle of sin people needed to be released from.

New Testament scholar Richard Horsley argues, "By pointing to the forgiveness of God as directly available, Jesus was exposing the religious means by which the social restrictions on the people were maintained.

Thus, instead of the people continuing to blame themselves for their suffering, they were freed for a resumption of a productive, cooperative life in their communities."[4]

When Jesus forgave others, he was rehumanizing those who had been dehumanized. The people Jesus healed now had certainty that the injustice occurring in their lives was not their own fault. Perhaps Jesus's declaration of forgiveness was undoing the psychological guilt that had worsened—or in some cases, even caused—their physical ailments. Jesus released them from the shackles of sin, which liberated them from endlessly looking inward for the causes of their suffering. They were now free to look outward at the society that marginalized them.

Every occasion of forgiveness in the ministry of Jesus was a revelation. It was a divine disclosure of God's perspective of the world. From this divine perspective, the people Jesus healed were free from guilt. This is why religious teachers condemned Jesus for forgiving people, accusing him of blasphemy. Jesus's forgiveness was a direct challenge to the way society placed all the guilt on the poor and sick. The alternative revelation that Jesus preached challenged the accepted social divisions of his day.

This is the power of forgiveness. Forgiveness releases us from the cycle of self-blame and shame that prevents us from noticing the ways we are abused and exploited by our society.

My friend C.J. is a therapist who works with people in low-income housing. In every session he witnesses the cycle of self-blame and shame in those who have been harmed most by the sin of society. After all, many people go to therapy to "fix themselves" because they're already convinced that they're the problem.

C.J.'s clients will often begin by talking about a personal struggle, but then briefly mention a larger societal issue as a small detail in their story. C.J. stops and encourages them to talk more about those details to allow them to see how much pressure those societal issues create in their lives.

One of C.J.'s clients was facing eviction and homelessness because her housing manager discovered her drug addiction and reported it to the police. C.J. and his client had a meeting with the housing authority to convince them that she wouldn't violate the lease again by using illegal substances.

Drug addiction is a health issue. It shouldn't be a criminal issue. And people shouldn't be forced into homelessness because of a health issue. And homelessness shouldn't be an issue at all when we can easily afford to house everyone in the country. This is the sin of society.

After the meeting, C.J. reminded his client that they're working through the situation to keep her housed and to make sure she doesn't break the rules that are in place. But then he expressed how much he wished she didn't have to be in this situation, and how much he wished the world we lived in didn't punish her for using drugs, and that her housing shouldn't be in jeopardy because of that. "This is inhumane that you are being treated this way because you have an addiction problem," he assured her.

This is the kind of forgiveness that Jesus gave. The sin of society always weighs on the poor and the sick. Jesus releases them from that pressure.

ALL THINGS ARE POSSIBLE

Forgiveness is excessive. It goes over and beyond. Forgiveness does not stop at releasing people at an interpersonal level. Forgiveness always moves outward to address the larger sin of society. It's common to see forgiveness transform individuals. Rarely do we see forgiveness transform a society. That requires a particularly excessive forgiveness that dares to believe in the impossible.

To get a grasp on this radically transformative forgiveness, we need to turn to the remarkable imaginations of the medieval theologians and recruit the help of an eleventh-century Italian theologian and Benedictine monk Peter Damian.

Peter Damian wrote an open letter to a friend titled *Letter on Divine Omnipotence* in 1065 after an earlier conversation about a passage from the theologian Jerome. Jerome had said that God cannot make a woman a virgin again after she had lost her virginity. His friend agreed. Damian disagreed.

This question was a part of an older speculative discussion among many Christians and non-Christians over the centuries: "Is God able to act so that, after something has once happened, it did not happen?"[5] Could God reach back into history and change the course of events? Could God erase events from history after they have already happened? This, of course, is not just a question about the power of God, but also about the mercy of God. This is a question about how much forgiveness can truly transform a situation. Could God's forgiveness transform history itself?

We all have had the desire to travel back in time and change things, whether it be preventing a genocide or something as small as changing the way we responded in a past conversation, like Peter Damian was doing in this letter.

He says he left the conversation dissatisfied, particularly with the conclusion that the all-powerful God was unable to do something. He argued that if God does not do something, it is simply because it is outside of God's will, but never because God is incapable. So he asserts that God is indeed "strong enough" to make a woman a virgin again.[6] He even argues that God could make it so that Rome had never been founded if God chose to do so.

He criticized those who get caught up in these speculative conversations about what God cannot do as "introducers of sacrilegious doctrine" and "secular boys" who, with their "dazzle of words," "tripped themselves up" with "frivolous questioning."[7]

These are age-old questions: "Could God create a stone so heavy that even God could not lift it?" or "Could God make a burrito so hot that even God could not eat it?" I imagine Peter Damian would respond to these questions by condemning them for a lack of faith and say, "Yes, of course God could lift that stone while eating that burrito."

He wasn't interested in trying to figure out what God *cannot* do. Jesus said, "for God all things are possible,"[8] and Peter Damian believed it.

I'm fascinated with Peter Damian's passionate argument, not because I am interested in defending the integrity of some all-powerful God. That's not important to me. I'm fascinated because I also find myself believing in the impossible. I believe in a forgiveness *so* transformative that it can reshape the world around us, but like Peter Damian, I am often frustrated with those around me who have a severe lack of imagination for what can and cannot be done.

I'm sure you've felt this way too. We demand health care for all, or housing for all, or education for all, but the "secular boys" of our day "trip themselves up" with "frivolous questioning" about who's going to pay for it. We demand the abolition of prisons and police, but they ask what we're going to do with all the "criminals." We demand an end to America's imperialism, but they ask what we're going to do if terrorists attack us.

Each of these questions is important to ask in order to have these discussions, but these questions are often inserted in order to shut the discussion down. Many people are not asking these questions sincerely. They ask these questions to cast doubt on a vision of radical transformation.

Like Peter Damian, I respond to these questions by declaring that *all things are possible.*

AS IF IT NEVER HAPPENED

John Caputo is also fascinated with Peter Damian's imaginative conception of forgiveness and speculates about the impact of what he calls *Forgiven Time.* He affirms that forgiveness "requires a past that ceases to be: in forgiveness it is to be as if it never happened." This is different from revisionist history, which attempts to sweep the past under the rug, believing it'll go away if we pretend it isn't there. "Forgiveness must somehow strike a blow against the past itself," he says. "The past would be somehow wiped out, annulled, or erased, so that, were it possible, it really would be the case that 'it never happened.'"[9]

The type of forgiveness that literally erases events from history is impossible, and yet, this is the level of transformation we should strive for when we talk about forgiveness. This is the level of release from the power of the past we should strive for.

Take, for example, the power of the past of white supremacy. If we want reconciliation after centuries of white supremacist violence and discrimination, then we should strive to reshape our material relations in such a way that our everyday lives appear as if white supremacy truly was erased from history.

We observe how people treat one another all the time. We know what it looks like when a relationship is broken and needs to be reconciled through people's subtle actions. But sometimes reconciliation has so transformed a situation that the relationship appears as if nothing happened.

Of course, there is an obvious difference between *pretending* nothing happened and restoring the relationship so much so that the relationship now flourishes as if nothing happened. Many of us have experienced the phony type of reconciliation where we are expected to pretend nothing happened, even though there is still harm being committed. Then, if you bring up the active harm, you are condemned for not "letting go" of the past like everyone else is trying to do.

This is often how people expect us to respond to centuries of white supremacy today. We are expected to pretend that the sins of the past never happened, even though the material relations of our everyday lives reflect a different reality. Then, when we acknowledge the ways that white supremacy still affects us, we are condemned for not "letting go" of the past. We're accused of keeping white supremacy alive by continuing to talk about it. This is similar to an abusive partner who apologizes after an act of abuse but still continues to harm their partner. If their partner brings up the endless pattern of abusive behavior, then they are accused of being "unforgiving" and blamed for their abuser's outbursts.

The most authentic reconciliation can occur only when the sins of the past are confronted and every wrong is made right. Often, it is impossible to achieve that level of reconciliation but that is what we should strive for, especially if we believe in the Christian story.

The New Testament speaks of history moving toward the restoration of all things,[10] the reconciliation of all things,[11] and the renewal of all things[12] through Christ. So the mission of the *body* of Christ should be to strive for the same type of radical transformation in response to brutal injustice.

With God all things are possible, right? And whatever proves to be impossible should not be the result of Christians refusing to attempt the impossible. Radical reparation of an unjust world should be our goal if we believe in something as radical as Christian forgiveness.

RADICAL RECONCILIATION

We see this level of expansive reconciliation in Jesus's classic parable of the prodigal son. In order to illustrate the kind of world he's talking about when he talks about "the kingdom of God," Jesus tells some stories about lost things being found. A shepherd with a hundred sheep loses one and leaves the ninety-nine to search until he finds the lost sheep, and then he invites his friends and neighbors over to celebrate. A woman with ten silver coins loses one and searches the entire house until she finds it, and then she invites her friends and neighbors over to celebrate.

Then Jesus tells a story of a son who asks his father for an early inheritance, and then leaves to a distant country and squanders it all. Then famine strikes the country, so he sells himself as a servant and ends up starving as he craves the food he's feeding to pigs. In this rock-bottom moment, he has a realization and thinks to himself: *How many of my father's hired hands have bread enough and to spare, but here I am dying of hunger! I will get up and go to my father, and I will say to him, "Father, I have sinned against heaven and before you; I am no longer worthy to be called your son; treat me like one of your hired hands."*[13] The father could continue holding the past over his son or he could release his son.

The story continues:

> So he set off and went to his father. But while he was still far off, his father saw him and was filled with compassion; he ran and put his arms around him and kissed him. Then the son said to him, "Father, I have sinned against heaven and before you; I am no longer worthy to be called your son." But the father said to his slaves, "Quickly, bring out a robe—the best one—and put

it on him; put a ring on his finger and sandals on his feet. And get the fatted calf and kill it, and let us eat and celebrate; for this son of mine was dead and is alive again; he was lost and is found!" And they began to celebrate.[14]

When the relationship needed to be reconciled, the father released his son from everything he held over him. But, of course, he doesn't stop there. The father seeks to right every wrong by transforming his son's conditions in a way that wipes out the past. The father repairs that which was broken so much so that it appears as if the relationship was never broken.

If the prodigal son returned as a servant, he would be reminded by his daily living conditions of the brokenness of his past, while the father continued to live in wealth and comfort. In that situation, the father could claim that he's forgotten the past, and maybe he would believe it himself, but the son's daily life would reflect a different reality.

The kind of repair that Christians should strive for requires a radical collective imagination, as well as radical collective action, to transform our world so that the wrongs of the past are made right. The restoration of all things, the reconciliation of all things, and the renewal of all things are what drives us.

Christians who believe in this level of transformation have a duty to look around at the injustice in our world today and to seek the most radically expansive methods of repairing all that is broken. Rarely do we see Christians who have the radical imagination for reconciliation and repair to the extent that Jesus talked about.

TRANSFORMATION REQUIRES REPARATIONS

We cannot talk about repair without addressing the call for economic reparations for Black Americans for the legacy of chattel slavery in the United States. Christians are called to commit to fulfilling this form of reparation as well, but it's an uncomfortable conversation because we've been trained to accept the phony type of reconciliation in which we pretend nothing happened. This is obviously a much easier task for the most privileged of society than the underprivileged.

It is a lot easier for the descendants of those who have always been in privileged positions in society to ignore everyday signs of brokenness than it is for the descendants of those who have been historically underprivileged because the signs of brokenness are reflected in their life conditions.

When people demand reparations, those who don't have a material need for reparations cannot immediately comprehend the needs of others. So often those with more privilege than others become angry and combative when people suggest any form of reparations because they foolishly believe *they're* the ones being oppressed when others are finally given the same privileges they've always enjoyed.

This plays out in the rest of the parable as well. The father's other son, the prodigal son's older brother, stayed with his father while his younger brother was absent. The story continues:

> Now his elder son was in the field; and when he came and approached the house, he heard music and dancing. He called one of the slaves and asked what was going on. He replied, "Your brother has come, and your father has killed the fatted calf, because he has got him back safe and sound." Then he became angry and refused to go in. His father came out and began to plead with him. But he answered his father, "Listen! For all these years I have been working like a slave for you, and I have never disobeyed your command; yet you have never given me even a young goat so that I might celebrate with my friends. But when this son of yours came back, who has devoured your property with prostitutes, you killed the fatted calf for him!" Then the father said to him, "Son, you are always with me, and all that is mine is yours. But we had to celebrate and rejoice, because this brother of yours was dead and has come to life; he was lost and has been found."[15]

Any form of reparations feels unfair to white people who can't see what has always been theirs. In a society that has historically favored white people, they must recognize that people of color are often fighting to have access to the same opportunities and freedoms that white people have always had access to. White privilege doesn't mean that every single white person is born with more wealth and resources than every single nonwhite person. We all struggle, including white working-class people. White privilege just means that white people's skin color isn't one of the factors that contribute to their struggle to survive in this society that dehumanizes all of us.

In our situation Black Americans have always been cast out, and for no fault of their own, unlike the prodigal son. A reconciliation would be a form of unity that has never existed before. And in our situation, there is no father that can restore anyone or orchestrate our reconciliation for us.

Those with the power to act justly cannot be persuaded to save us. The problem is that the power to act justly rests in the hands of so few. The solution is not to persuade the powerful, but to transform our entire socioeconomic system so that power is more equally distributed among all of us. This is part of the ongoing work of reparation as well. Liberation is achieved when our communities have the power to fulfill our needs ourselves.

Liberation cannot come from above, only from below. The oppressed struggle for power to free themselves from oppression and within this struggle God chooses the side of the oppressed. Christians are called to embody the God of the oppressed in the world, struggling alongside the oppressed for liberation.

CHEAP FORGIVENESS

What are we really working toward? Are we working toward the kind of transformation that Jesus talked about? Are we working toward a complete release of everything held over the oppressed? Are we working to repair our world to reflect a new reality?

Or are we settling for a phony reconciliation that demands people reconcile with their enemies while they are still being abused and exploited by them?

Are we working toward the type of forgiveness that empowers us to resist unjust institutions? Or are we settling for a cheap forgiveness that suppresses our resistance?

On May 25, 2020, in Minneapolis, Minnesota, George Floyd was murdered by police when Officer Derek Chauvin pressed his knee into Floyd's neck for nine minutes and twenty-nine seconds. The next day, protests began and gradually spread throughout the world within a week. Multiple protests in the United States lasted several months, night after night.

A couple of weeks after protests began, the popular right-wing evangelical worship leader Sean Feucht brought a worship team to hold a concert and outreach event at the site of George Floyd's murder where protests were taking place. They sang worship songs, preached, prayed for people, and baptized people in big plastic containers. All this took place a few yards away from the mural at the site of George Floyd's murder.

When I saw the videos online, all I could think of was the scripture Amos 5 where God uses the prophet Amos to tell Israel: "Away with the noise of your songs! I will not listen to the music of your harps. But let justice roll on like a river, righteousness like a never-failing stream!"[16] It's common in the prophetic books of the Hebrew Bible for God to condemn Israel for prioritizing worship over justice. This sin is more prevalent than ever today.

One of the musicians praised the event for helping people turn to forgiveness in Jesus and understand that Jesus—not a protest— is the answer. The obvious implication was that the protest was the *real* problem, and that the solution to the unrest would be for protesters to forgive the police by forgetting about the injustice around them.

The only type of forgiveness many Christians are interested in is pressuring oppressed people to release the resentment they may hold over oppressive institutions. The type of forgiveness I'm interested in is America releasing the oppression they hold over everyone struggling to survive state violence. That necessarily means reparations. And the type of reparations I'm talking about includes the abolition of institutions that were built to sustain the oppression we claim to have ended centuries ago. That includes the abolition of prisons. That includes the abolition of police. That even includes the abolition of capitalism, which was only made financially viable in the United

States by importing a working class from Africa through slavery.

This is why it's necessary we talk about forgiveness as *release*.

To forgive someone is to set them free to live beyond what was held over them. Forgiveness could look like releasing someone from the resentment you held over them as we commonly think of it, but it also can look like releasing someone from a debt you held over them, no longer requiring payment. The important part is the release, and forgiveness functions as a cycle of release.

Reconciliation occurs when forgiveness so transforms a situation that the oppressor releases the victim from their mistreatment and the oppressed releases the oppressor from their resentment. Reconciliation occurs when both parties are released. Until both parties are released, reconciliation cannot be achieved.

If you want oppressed people to release the resentment they hold over their oppressors, then release them from their oppression. How could you forgive a friend for pressing their boot into your neck if your friend still hasn't lifted their boot? You could say that you've forgiven and forgotten it, but it won't really matter until the oppression stops.

RADICAL CHANGE

In Matthew 18, Peter asks Jesus, "Lord, if another member of the church sins against me, how often should I forgive? As many as seven times?" Jesus replied, "Not seven times, but, I tell you, seventy-seven times."[17]

Biblical scholars argue that the reason Jesus told Peter to forgive seventy-seven times in Matthew 18 is because the writer, Matthew, was making a correction on an evolving Christian teaching on forgiveness. Both Luke and Matthew document this Christian teaching on forgiveness separately. Luke 17 records Jesus saying, "And if the same person sins against you seven times a day, and turns back to you seven times and says, 'I repent,' you must forgive."[18] This was likely a common teaching among the early Christian community that taught people to forgive people seven times as a way of making the point that we should endlessly forgive. Then what likely happened is that people took this teaching literally and began teaching that we only need to forgive people seven times and no more after that. So Matthew corrects this misunderstanding by writing this story about Peter asking Jesus if we should forgive seven times, and Jesus responds, "Not seven times, but, I tell you, seventy-seven times."

This is what we often do with radical teachings such as this. We find a way to avoid its excessive nature and create rules and restrictions to avoid following the teaching beyond what's convenient. We cling to the safety of our familiar worldviews to avoid the challenge of radical change.

And yet, the restoration of all things, the reconciliation of all things, and the renewal of all things require nothing less than radical change.

In Luke's version of the story, the apostles respond to Jesus's teaching on forgiveness by saying, "Increase our faith!" May we be humble enough to also pray for an increase of faith as we commit to transforming the world in such a radically expansive way.

6

ABOLITION COME, ON EARTH AS IT IS IN HEAVEN

When I began my journey in church ministry, my goal was to plant a church so that I could teach and preach helpful and creative messages about Jesus and faith to as many people as possible. Then I started talking to pastors about how they planted their churches. Some pastors exhibited the kind of ministry I was interested in as they talked about attracting people to their church by preaching a unique message.

Then I started meeting pastors who talked about serving their cities and partnering with organizations that gave their local communities the care and resources they needed. When I first heard this, I naively processed these ideas of serving the community as another cool way to get people to go to your church to hear your message. The particular type of ministry environment I was involved in taught me to process everything that way. It took me a while to realize that these specific pastors really cared about their cities and wanted to dedicate their ministries to caring for their local communities.

They weren't talking about running a Sunday service while helping in the community every once in a while. They were talking about opening community centers that just happened to also have service on Sundays. When I discovered this way of thinking about church, it changed the way I thought about everything.

Jesus taught about the kingdom of God more than anything, and those verses were more about a unique way of life than a unique message. The English translation of the Greek *basileia tou Theou* into the "kingdom of God" is too ambiguous, especially considering our common associations with the word kingdom. *King* is too patriarchal and forces us to imagine a man on a throne, but this isn't what Jesus was talking about. And -dom sounds like a physical location you could visit. This isn't what Jesus was talking about either.

The word *basileia* is better translated "reign," or "rule," or "power." A king has basileia over a physical location, but his basileia isn't the location itself. You can't see basileia. You can only experience it.

So the basileia of God, or the reign of God, is referring to what the world would be like with God in charge. Jesus and his fellow Jews believed that the reign of Rome was coming to an end, and a new reign was emerging. This new reign, however, did not just look like the old reign with a new person on the throne. The reign of God describes an alternative use of power. When Jesus described this reign, he described liberation.

Jesus said the reign of God belonged to the poor and the persecuted.[1] He said many will come from east and west to be a part of the reign of God.[2] He went city to city teaching people to repent, or rather, to transform their lives because the reign of God is at hand.[3] Preparing for the reign of God looks like choosing to live differently in the world. It looks like living as if the reign of God is already here.

Many Christians may instinctively assume the reign of God is referring to heaven, but Jesus isn't talking about the afterlife. For Jesus, the reign of God is an emerging reality right here and right now. Jesus says the reign of God is within you.[4] He also compares the reign of God to a tiny mustard seed that grows into a large tree.[5] And he compares it to yeast that grows into leavened bread.[6] The reign of God is something that starts out small within us and then grows through us and out into the world.

Jesus taught people how to live differently so that others would know through observing their lifestyle that the reign of God is present. Jesus teaches his disciples to pray, "Your kingdom come. Your will be done, on earth as it is in heaven."[7] The mission of Jesus's followers is not to simply *believe* in the reign of God, but to participate in the process of materializing the reign of God here on Earth.

The reign of God was not a purely utopian vision of a perfect world, free from any sort of struggle. The early advocates for the reign of God did imagine that kind of utopia sometime in the future, but a utopia is not what motivated their solutions. Their solutions were not motivated by an ideal of perfection. Their solutions were motivated by the actual problems they were experiencing in society.

In Jesus's first sermon in Luke 4, he quoted the prophet Isaiah and says the spirit of the Lord anointed him "to bring good news to the poor . . . proclaim release to the captives and recovery of sight to the blind, to let the oppressed go free, to proclaim the year of the Lord's favor."[8] When John the Baptist sent messengers to Jesus to confirm if Jesus was the one to come, Jesus responded, "Go and tell John what you have seen and heard: the blind receive their sight, the lame walk, the lepers are cleansed, the deaf hear, the dead are raised, the poor have good news brought to them."[9] Jesus knew that John wasn't checking on his doctrine. John wanted to confirm that Jesus was materializing the reign of God through healing the sick and aiding the oppressed.

The church in Acts continued Jesus's healing work, but they also developed local communities where they shared all things in common and redistributed money and resources to those who had need. This is what living out the reign of God looks like.

Jesus said the last will be first and the first will be last in the reign of God.[10] The reign of God is a direct challenge to the socioeconomic structure of society, promising to radically transform society so much so that the power dynamics would be directly flipped upside down. The French West Indian postcolonial theorist and activist Frantz Fanon quoted Jesus saying the first will be last and the last will be first to describe what decolonization looks like in practice.[11]

The early Christians lived this alternative lifestyle because they were certain that the current socioeconomic structure of Rome was about to end. They did not believe the reign of God would reform the reign of Rome. The reign of God referred to the way we live after Rome is destroyed. It turned out that Rome lasted a lot longer than they expected. And when Rome finally fell centuries later, more empires took power throughout history and continued oppressing those who Jesus seeks to liberate.

So living out the reign of God today means living alternatively to whatever empire we find ourselves in. We do not seek to reform oppressive institutions.

We seek alternative solutions and care for our communities so that we may survive the inevitable abolition of our oppressive institutions.

ABOLITION DEMOCRACY

Christians who want to materialize the reign of God on earth today must reflect on what Jesus meant when he spoke of the last becoming first and the first becoming last. We must determine what that flip in the power dynamic looks like in our current society. What institutions exist to maintain that divide between the first and the last? What institutions would Jesus seek to abolish in order for the reign of God to emerge?

When we understand the ways that white supremacy still functions institutionally, we see how much still needs to be repaired. Monetary reparations to Black Americans for chattel slavery would simply be a good start. Those who seek to truly transform our society to repair all that is broken demand much more than that. We must also recognize other institutions that have maintained racial divisions to this day, such as the prison–industrial complex (PIC).

Critical Resistance, one of many organizations that fight to end the PIC, defines the PIC on their website as "the overlapping interests of government and industry that use surveillance, policing, and imprisonment as solutions to economic, social, and political problems." They go on to define PIC abolition as "a political vision with the goal of eliminating imprisonment, policing, and surveillance and creating lasting alternatives to punishment and imprisonment."[12]

Eliminating imprisonment, policing, and surveillance may initially sound like a huge leap in a conversation about reparations for chattel slavery, but this is part of a larger effort to repair what has been broken through centuries of colonialism and white supremacy. As political activist and philosopher Angela Davis explains, it is clear that there is "an unbroken stream of racist violence, both official and extralegal, from slave patrols and the Ku Klux Klan to contemporary profiling practices and present-day vigilantes."[13]

Angela Davis argues,

> There is a direct connection with slavery: when slavery was abolished, black people were set free, but they lacked access to the material resources that would enable them to fashion new, free lives. Prisons have thrived over the last century precisely because of the absence of those resources and the persistence of some of the deep structures of slavery. They cannot, therefore, be eliminated unless new institutions and resources are made available to those communities that provide, in large part, the human beings that make up the prison population.[14]

The commitment to building new institutions and resources is a commitment to the old and unfinished work of "abolition democracy," a term Angela Davis uses in her book of the same name, taking after W. E. B. Du Bois. Du Bois used this term in 1935 when writing about the Black Reconstruction era that began in 1867. This reconstruction effort was aborted in 1877, leaving the reconstruction of Black communities unfinished. Angela Davis explains that "a host of democratic institutions are needed to fully achieve abolition—thus abolition democracy."[15]

The absence of chattel slavery was not enough. The failure to create new democratic institutions to provide formerly enslaved people and their descendants with economic subsistence left the work of abolition incomplete. The PIC was invented to maintain the inequality that abolition was attempting to solve, so abolition democracy requires the abolition of the PIC too.

A popular claim is that racism is still alive in the United States primarily because of the people who are still talking about racism. Turn on the news or check social media and you'll hear people say we are more divided than ever, and that this division is one of the biggest problems we face. They are right when they say that we are greatly divided. However, this division is caused by the alienation that is maintained by unjust institutions, not by us talking about it.

People claim in public discourse on these issues that those who are trying to abolish our divisive institutions are actually causing the division. Their theory is that these divisions will go away if we simply stop thinking and talking about them so much. This is what the justification of white supremacy often looks like today. It is not always through obvious bigoted statements, but also through demands for unity and peace without justice and liberation.

BLACK LIVES MATTER

So when a Black person is murdered by the police and people respond with protests in the streets, then we must recognize that these protests are not solely a response to the specific murder, but to the "unbroken stream of racist violence" that the murder represents. The recent increase in protests against police violence is not because of an increase in police violence, but because of an increase in the ease of publicly sharing video footage of police violence on social media.

Alicia Garza, cofounder of the Black Lives Matter movement in 2013, describes the movement as a tactic to rebuild the Black liberation movement. She says,

> When we say Black Lives Matter, we are talking about the ways in which Black people are deprived of our basic human rights and dignity. It is an acknowledgment Black poverty and genocide is state violence. It is an acknowledgment that 1 million Black people are locked in cages in this country–one half of all people in prisons or jails–is an act of state violence.[16]

When we ask about how we can repair that which was broken through centuries of white supremacy, about how we can bring an end to "the stream of racist violence," about how we can heal our racial divisions and reconcile as a society, then we must listen to those who are calling for a radical transformation. If we claim that some activists are "going too far" or demanding "too much" or "too fast," then we must ask ourselves if we truly have the radical imagination we need.

THE PURPOSE OF THE POLICE

While many activists in the Black Lives Matter movement are fighting for a reformation of the PIC, many activists are also fighting for total abolition. Those fighting for abolition interpret the term "police violence" as redundant, claiming that the purpose of police is inherently violent. Many people become abolitionists after witnessing the failure of police reform again and again. Reformist policies often lead to increased police budgets to fulfill those policies, but increased police budgets often lead to increased police violence, causing an endless cycle.

In the reign of God, the last will be first and the first will be last. Materializing the reign of God looks like flipping the power dynamic, empowering the poor and the oppressed to take back power that was meant to belong to all of us.

The police force was invented two hundred years ago for the purpose of making sure this flip in the power dynamic never takes place.

The first official police department was founded in London in 1829, created and funded by business owners to control the crowds of striking workers with nonlethal violence so as not to create working-class martyrs that could lead to further riots. New York adopted this strategy in 1844 with teams of white citizen volunteers to manage the disorder of the strikes and protect business owners' property. They also adopted strategies of the slave patrols of the South, which had existed since 1783 and were founded to prevent slave revolts through constant surveillance and harassment. As civil unrest increased, the budget, the power, and therefore the violence of the volunteer watch increased, culminating in the formation of the New York Police Department in 1845.

In the South, slave patrols evolved into police forces. After the abolition of chattel slavery, the South created "Black codes" that criminalized unemployment and turned various misdemeanors into felonies, transforming newly freed Black communities from an enslaved class into a criminalized class, coerced into slave labor once again in prisons.

Slavery was never fully abolished in the United States. It just evolved into the PIC, profiting off the labor of the imprisoned.

While this summary only skims the surface of the history of the evolution of policing and prisons, we can confirm that as wealth inequality has increased, civil unrest has increased, which has led to the state responding as they always have, by increasing policing and prisons. So even though policing has evolved in many ways over the centuries, the purpose of policing remains the same: social control.

The mission of the PIC is antithetical to the mission of the reign of God because the mission of the reign of God is to cultivate a world in which the last become first and the first become last, while historically, the mission of the PIC has been to protect and serve the interests of the first in society so that they remain first while the last remain last.

It is no coincidence that those who have the most motivation to abolish our unjust institutions are the most heavily policed and imprisoned. Sociologist Alex Vitale explains that police spend the vast majority of their time on patrol, which has been known to target mostly poor neighborhoods and people of color, "based on a mindset that people of color commit more crime and therefore must be subjected to harsher police tactics."

Police argue that residents in high-crime communities often demand police action. What is left out is that these communities also ask for better schools, parks, libraries, and jobs, but these services are rarely provided. They lack the political power to obtain real services and support to make their communities safer and healthier. The reality is that middle-class and wealthy white communities would put a stop to the constant harassment and humiliation meted out by police in communities of color, no matter the crime rate.[17]

Our historical strategy for solving social problems has been suppression through violent social control. We must create alternatives that actually help us instead of further harming us. The goal of abolition is the development of new institutions that keep our communities safe and healthy so that we no longer need to turn to state violence to solve our problems.

Abolitionist organizer Mariame Kaba encourages us to ask new questions. Instead of asking, *Does this mean that I can never call the cops if my life is in serious danger?* we should ask, *Why do we have no other well-resourced options?* Instead of asking, *What do we have now, and how can we make it better?* we should ask, *What can we imagine for ourselves and the world?*[18]

Conversations about abolition often lead to someone anxiously asking, "Well what do we do about murders, sexual assaults, and burglaries?" while ignoring the fact that police do not *prevent* murders, sexual assaults, and burglaries. The police are called after those crimes have been committed. Also, many people I know who are advocates for abolition have called the police after a murder, sexual assault, or burglary, and the police were either unable to do anything about it, or made the situation even more violent and traumatic. A more honest conversation about abolition begins with asking about alternative solutions besides state violence. It's about collective organizing to create new institutions that adequately resource communities.

The truth is, the element most often linked to changing crime rates is not the rate of punishment by the state, but the rate of poverty. When poverty decreases, crime decreases. Instead of acknowledging this key fact we keep increasing police budgets, expecting it to work with no justifiable reason to.

Many of these conversations are cut short when someone throws their hands up and claims that organizing toward abolition is too extreme and impractical. This reaction is understandable, considering how stifled our imaginations are by pro-PIC propaganda, but frankly, I expect much more imagination from Christians. If you believe we are called to materialize the reign of God here on Earth, then you expose yourself as hypocritical when you dismiss radical alternatives for justice as too impractical. If we're committed to the radical upside-down vision of the reign of God, then how could any alternatives be too impractical?

PROPHETIC PESSIMISM

Abolitionists are often accused of being too pessimistic, and I may sound pretty pessimistic myself. When an abolitionist rejects ideas for incremental change, it could sound like they aren't interested in change at all. A pessimistic attitude that discourages us from making *any* changes should be avoided at all costs. However, there is another kind of pessimism that we desperately need. This pessimism empowers us to do something radically different from what we are familiar with. After all, optimism for a new world begins with pessimism about the world in its current form.

In a surprisingly crucial way, the difficult work of building the world we hope for begins with "embracing hopelessness," as the theologian Miguel De La Torre speaks of in his book of the same name. He criticizes hope as "a middle-class privilege," arguing that it

> soothes the conscience of those complicit with oppressive structures, lulling them to do nothing except look forward to a salvific future where every wrong will be righted and every tear wiped away, while numbing themselves to the pain of those oppressed, lest that pain motivate them to take radical action.[19]

This pain that motivates radical action is present in the hopeless pessimism of the Hebrew prophets, who did not call for the empires that oppressed them to reform, but to be destroyed. Jesus and his followers tap into this prophetic pessimism and imagine the emergence of the reign of God as dependent on the destruction of the reign of Rome.

Mary taps into this old prophetic pessimism as well at the beginning of Luke's Gospel. After she discovers she is pregnant with Jesus she praises God in a prayer, later known as the Magnificat. In the middle of this praise she says of God, "He has brought down the powerful from their thrones, and lifted up the lowly; he has filled the hungry with good things, and sent the rich away empty."[20]

These lines are inspired by various Hebrew scriptures that capture a similar theme, such as 1 Samuel 2:7–8: "The Lord makes poor and makes rich; he brings low, he also exalts. He raises up the poor from the dust; he lifts the needy from the ash heap, to make them sit with princes and inherit a seat of honor"; Sirach 10:14: "The Lord overthrows the thrones of rulers, and enthrones the lowly in their place"; and Job 12:19: "He leads priests away stripped, and overthrows the mighty."

The vision of change that Mary adopts as she praises God is an uncomfortably violent one. For Mary, the lifting up of the lowly is unavoidably linked to the destruction of the powerful. You can't have one without the other.

If you were to ask Mary about the kind of change she wanted, she would say that the powerful are brought down from their thrones and the rich are sent away empty. You may discourage her pessimism and encourage her to have more hope, but she would remind you that her hope is in the lowly being lifted and the hungry being fed. And she would remind you that it would only happen by the powerful being brought down. Mary did not hope that Roman society would implement the right reforms to reduce harm.

Mary had no hope in the Roman Empire getting better. Mary is an abolitionist, not a reformist. Mary is a revolutionary.

You may struggle to relate to this radical hopelessness, but think about the ways hopelessness has set you free before. You may have thought an abusive relationship could get better, but then one day you realized the only healthy option was to end it. You may have struggled to stay a part of a local church, hoping your leaders would do better, but then one day you lost hope in them changing, and you left. You may have had some sort of worldview you used to force on others, thinking everyone's lives would be better if they just thought the way you thought, but then one day you realized you were wrong, and let it go. You lose hope in these things because you realize your hope is in something larger. Your hope is no longer in things getting better, but in the creation of something new.

We are often quick to dismiss the pessimism that sees no hope in reform, but if we truly want radical change we must listen to these critiques. We must listen to the desperation for something new.

THE TRANSFORMATIVE TIME OF THE REIGN OF GOD

Rose Braz, cofounder of Critical Resistance, said in an interview, "A prerequisite to seeking any social change is the naming of it. In other words, even though the goal we seek may be far away, unless we name it and fight for it today, it will never come."[21]

The reign of God functions in a similar way. You look around at the world in the first century and the twenty-first century, and it's obvious that the world is not ruled by the liberation of God. The reign of God is a vision of the world to come, but we embody this alternative way of life right here and right now, even while living under a reign that we reject. Keeping that ambitious vision in view on the horizon empowers us to keep working toward it.

This is about a different relationship with time. Sociologist Avery Gordon talks about abolitionists keeping transformative time.

> Abolition recognizes that transformative time doesn't always stop the world, as if in an absolute break between now and then, but is a daily part of it, a way of being in the ongoing work of emancipation, a work which inevitably must take place while you're still enslaved, imprisoned, indebted, occupied, walled in, commodified, etc.[22]

As I talk about the similarities between Jesus's vision of the reign of God and the vision of abolition, I am not trying to force a Christian meaning onto the work of abolition or suggest that the work of abolition is really just the work of the reign of God without abolitionists realizing it. I'm saying that the best way Christians can fulfill the work of the reign of God today is to participate in the work of abolition. And by participating in the ongoing work of abolition, we gain a fresh understanding of the type of liberation Jesus talked about.

Abolitionist organizers Dan Berger, Mariame Kaba, and David Stein describe the daily work of abolition as fighting "to reduce state violence and maximize people's collective well-being." They write,

> Abolitionists have worked to end solitary confinement and the death penalty, stop the construction of new prisons, eradicate cash bail, organized to free people from prison, opposed the expansion of punishment through hate crime laws and surveillance, pushed for universal health care, and developed alternative modes of conflict resolution that do not rely on the criminal punishment system.[23]

The only reforms worth supporting are reforms that fund our communities and give more power to the people in them. Supporting reforms that give more funding and power to the PIC keeps the violent cycle going. We need better solutions to social problems, and that requires us being open to solutions that we've never considered before.

Jesus encouraged his followers to materialize the reign of God on earth right here and right now. That materialization is dependent on the abolition of the unjust institutions that maintain our divisions. The

Christianity of this land preserves these institutions, while the Christianity of Christ demands their abolition. Abolition is just about the most Christian thing we can do.

7

THE OBEDIENT, UNRIGHTEOUS SON

My friend Kyle grew up in a conservative evangelical church in Florida. He was told since he was a child that he was spiritually gifted and called to ministry. As a teenager, he joined the church's adults on trips to the local jail and prison to talk and pray with people. He also volunteered with his church to feed the homeless once a month.

Over time, tensions rose as he began noticing signs that he was taking his faith more seriously than his church expected him to. He wondered why the church only fed the homeless once a month since he was buying lunches for homeless people on his own more often than that. He also wanted to feed homeless people without being required to try to convert them to Christianity, especially because many of them were already Christians. He also became discouraged seeing people at his church mock and insult strippers at the strip club by his work while preaching about Jesus, who befriended sex workers and other marginalized people commonly excluded by religious people.

"I read the fucking footnotes!" Kyle passionately told me as he talked about reading the Bible and discovering the differences between the radical life of Jesus and the hypocritical lives of those around him. It wasn't that he didn't have enough faith, but that he had as much faith as humanly possible before realizing his faith was in something that doesn't work.

Discovering that he was gay made following this path of evangelical ministry even more difficult. Gay people were one of the several marginalized groups his church discriminated against.

In college Kyle changed schools as he attempted to rediscover himself and his life's path. He met some radical Christians who served people in need, not as a means to an end like he experienced growing up, but as an end in itself. These were the kinds of Christians he wished he grew up with, but eventually this desire to help people led Kyle out of Christian communities and into political advocacy groups. With half a religious studies degree, he gradually stopped attending church, stopped believing in the God he grew up with, and discovered a new passion in advocating for workers through organizing labor unions. He says it feels like he's finally playing offense. Over the years his politics became more radical, he married his husband, and he started a local chapter for the Industrial Workers of the World, a worker-led international labor union.

Kyle's story is fascinating to me because we can view the trajectory of his life in one of two ways. From the perspective of the version of God he and I grew up with, it's a story of a man who started out passionately following God and living out his calling, but over time he started to go astray. Then he gave into his "homosexual desires" and really went off the rails. Now, as a Communist labor organizer, he couldn't be further from God as he leads other people astray with secular ideologies in this sad story of a fall from grace.

Then I think of the God of the Exodus, who freed the Israelites from slavery. And I think of Jesus, when he quotes the prophet Isaiah and announces his mission to bring good news to the poor, proclaim release to the captives, restore sight to the blind, and to let the oppressed go free. From the perspective of *that* God, Kyle has been on one long path of fulfilling the work of liberation that was planted in his heart as a child while serving people with his church. From that perspective Kyle followed God out of the church and into the world to help people who have no one to advocate for them.

This story reveals a common pattern in the lives of those who choose to take their faith seriously enough to take it to its radical conclusions. They fully embrace the teachings they heard from the church about sacrificial love and service to the world, and then those teachings lead them out of the church that raised them. Then they end up leading lives of radical political advocacy, which often positions them against their Christian peers, who seem to be uninterested in letting their faith lead them beyond the walls of the church. If this story sounds familiar, it's because this happens to a lot of us. You are not alone.

TRANSFORMING THE WHOLE ROAD

One year before he was assassinated, Dr. Martin Luther King Jr. gave a speech at Riverside Church in New York City, entitled "*Beyond Vietnam*." In addition to opposing the Vietnam War, he criticized "the giant triplets of racism, extreme materialism, and militarism." He advocated for a "revolution of values" to solve these issues. Then he said something I often come back to, and it's something I wish every Christian in the world would take seriously.

A true revolution of values will soon cause us to question the fairness and justice of many of our past and present policies. On the one hand, we are called to play the Good Samaritan on life's roadside, but that will be only an initial act. One day we must come to see that the whole Jericho Road must be transformed so that men and women will not be constantly

beaten and robbed as they make their journey on life's high-
way. True compassion is more than flinging a coin to a beggar.
It comes to see that an edifice which produces beggars needs
restructuring.[1]

The parable of the Good Samaritan is one of Jesus's
most famous parables.[2] A man is beaten, robbed, and
left half dead on the side of the road on the way to Jericho. A priest passes by and does nothing. A Levite—a
descendant of Israelites who had a special role in facil-
itating Jewish offerings—passes by and also does nothing. These are the two people you would expect to be
eager to help someone in need.

Then a Samaritan passes by. Jews and Samaritans had
a long and violent cultural rivalry, so the Samaritan was
the last person Jesus's disciples expected to stop and
help. And yet, as the parable goes, the Samaritan "was
moved with pity." The Samaritan cared for the man,
bandaged his wounds, carried him on an animal, and
paid for a room at the inn where the man could stay.

Identity does not determine goodness, and goodness
transcends identity.

This parable is also used to inspire us to be coura-
geously compassionate by helping others in need, even
when others won't. Most Christians have heard this
message before. Countless sermons have been preached
about the importance of helping poor individuals "on
life's roadside." However, King insists that helping individuals you pass by should only be "the initial act" if you

want to end their suffering. True compassion should lead us to address the systemic issues that cause the suffering of people you pass by.

Churches will give to charity every day but never question why so many people need charity. If you keep helping people beaten on the side of the road, you would be foolish to not ask why people keep getting beaten on the side of the road. If you keep giving to beggars, you would be foolish to not ask why our society keeps producing beggars.

It's dangerous to consider questions like this because it threatens the power dynamics of the current world. Brazilian Catholic Archbishop Helder Camara is famous for having said, "When I give food to the poor, they call me a saint. When I ask why they are poor, they call me a Communist."

Some of the Christians who asked these questions have literally become Communists as they sought to transform a society that produces so much poverty. In 1979 in Nicaragua, the Sandinista National Liberation Front overthrew the Somoza dictatorship through guerrilla warfare. Catholic priest and poet Ernesto Cardenal, one of my heroes, supported the Sandinistas and took part in their revolution, leading to Cardenal's election as the minister of culture for Nicaragua's new revolutionary government. As the Sandinistas worked to democratize the country in brand-new ways, Cardenal's role was to democratize art and culture. He drove the development of various cultural workshops, including a literacy initiative, which taught five hundred thousand Nicaraguans how to read and write.

In 1983, Pope John Paul II visited Cardenal and publicly rebuked him upon his arrival at the Managua airport. You can find photos and video footage online of Cardenal kneeling and looking up at the pope with a smile as the pope wags his finger sternly at Cardenal. "You must fix your affairs with the church," the pope demanded. Clergy are forbidden from assuming public office according to the Canon Law of the Catholic Church. However, this wasn't just about the technicalities of canon law. The pope was also committed to eliminating all forms of Communist influence in the church, and that meant condemning Latin American liberation theologians, like Cardenal, for collaborating with Marxists.

TWO UNRIGHTEOUS SONS

Most people don't know what to do with the idea of Catholic priests working with Marxists. But in the midst of intolerable poverty, Marxism offered a socioeconomic analysis of the exploitation at the root of poverty. For Marxists it all came down to who owned and controlled the means of producing and distributing goods and services. As long as a small class of owners owns and controls everything workers make, inequality will always exist. This contradiction is solved through workers transforming their workplaces and taking control. Private ownership is solved through collective ownership of the means of production to facilitate the equal distribution of resources.

Whether you agree with this solution or not, consider this. The church should have already been critiquing class inequality in Latin America and working to eliminate their exploitation, but instead the church justified their unjust conditions as the will of God.

So when Christians in Latin America were unable to tolerate their exploitation, the only other people who were speaking to their desire for justice were Marxists. They didn't replace their Christian faith with Marxism but used Marxist analysis as a tool for understanding socioeconomic problems. Some say Latin American Christians were tricked into believing Marxist ideas by outside agitators from the Soviet Union, or some other dubious source, but that conspiracy theory is often rooted in the bigoted trope that marginalized people can't think for themselves. It also ignores the fact that poverty itself is often the biggest culprit in radicalizing people to join revolutionary struggles against inequality.

In the early 1970s, the Brazilian Catholic priest Frei Betto was arrested, tortured, and imprisoned by Brazil's military dictatorship for his activism, along with the Marxist guerrilla fighter Carlos Marighella. The police interrogator asked Betto, "How can a Christian collaborate with a Communist?"[3]

Betto replied, "For me, men are divided not into believers and atheists, but between oppressors and oppressed, between those who want to keep this unjust society and those who want to struggle for justice."

The interrogator shot back, "Have you forgotten that Marx considered religion to be the opium of the people?"

Betto insisted, "It is the bourgeoisie which has turned religion into an opium of the people by preaching a God lord of the heavens only, while taking possession of the earth for itself."

I am reminded of a parable Jesus tells in Matthew 21 as he's teaching in the temple. The chief priests and elders begin challenging Jesus's authority and Jesus responds with a couple of parables, beginning with one about two sons:

> "What do you think? A man had two sons; he went to the first and said, 'Son, go and work in the vineyard today.' He answered, 'I will not'; but later he changed his mind and went. The father went to the second and said the same; and he answered, 'I go, sir'; but he did not go. Which of the two did the will of his father?" They said, "The first." Jesus said to them, "Truly I tell you, the tax collectors and the prostitutes are going into the kingdom of God ahead of you."[4]

This is a provocative story. A father tells one son to work in the vineyard, the son says no, but then later does it anyway. The father tells the other son to work in the vineyard, the son says yes, but never did it. In a culture that centered honor and shame in relationships, it is clear that both sons brought shame to their father. One brought shame by disobeying his father and the other, in spite of doing what his father asked, still brought shame on his father by rejecting his command. So when Jesus asks which of the two did the will of his father, this is not a question about which son is morally righteous. *Neither* son is. Jesus is asking which of the unrighteous sons ultimately did what the father asked. There is only one correct answer. It's the son who said he wouldn't work in the field but did it anyway.

Jesus uses this parable to condemn the chief priests and elders. By society's standards, the chief priests and elders were far more righteous than the tax collectors and the prostitutes. However, the question is not about who is more righteous, and the assumption is that both parties are unrighteous. The question is about who is doing the will of God. Jesus says he sees tax collectors and prostitutes doing the will of God before the chief priests and elders, which naturally makes them seek Jesus's arrest.

Many Christians who grow up in fundamentalist environments begin questioning what they are taught when they are confronted with its contradictions. One of the most striking contradictions is the realization that a group of people whom your church calls bad are actually not that bad after all. This group may be the stoners, the gang members, the gay kids, the partygoers, and all the non-Christians. But when you interact with these groups, you are surprised to discover that some of them seem to live by even higher moral ideals than you and your Christian friends. That discovery is earth-shattering to a young fundamentalist. You begin to notice that the compassionate and liberating way of Jesus is being lived out even more effectively by some of your non-Christian friends than by the Christians you know.

We encounter a similar inversion in this parable. There are people who reject the message but still follow the mission. And there are people who embrace the message but do not follow the mission. There are non-Christians living a more Christlike life than many Christians you know. The reason for this inversion is twofold: first, the failure of Christianity to live up to its calling; and second, people committing to the work of liberation from all kinds of perspectives because liberation is so desperately needed.

The point is not to say that non-Christians who follow the work of liberation are actually Christians without realizing it. That interpretation erases the diverse perspectives and motivations that compel people to work for liberation, and also enforces Christian hegemony by defining people in Christian terms against their will.

The parable wasn't for the tax collectors and the prostitutes. It was meant for the chief priests and elders.

This specific message isn't meant to give Christians permission to call non-Christians Christian. It's meant to expand the perspective of Christians, so they may discover that there are many people—even those you may consider unrighteous—who are fulfilling God's work of liberation. So following the work of liberation yourself will often look like joining forces with all kinds of different people from all kinds of different perspectives, perhaps even Marxist guerrilla fighters.

I imagine Jesus would look at the problems of poverty and unfair distribution and tell the Latin American priests who justified that injustice, "The Marxists are going into the kingdom of God ahead of you." If you find that offensive, then you have an idea of how the chief priests and elders felt after hearing Jesus's parable.

WHO DID THE WORK?

When we widen our perspectives in this way, our faith is challenged to grow, especially when we see non-Christians fulfill the work that Christians have said yes to but won't do.

In 1969, the Young Lords, a New York Puerto Rican street gang turned radical political organization, asked the First Spanish United Methodist Church if they could use their building to run a breakfast program and a day care center for the local children. The church was in the middle of the neighborhood and sat locked up and empty every day except for a few hours on Sunday.

The church said no. After weeks of the Young Lords attending services and being ignored, tensions culminated during a testimony service where members of the church could speak to the congregation. When Felipe Luciano, chairman of the Young Lords, stood up to speak, police rushed in and brutally beat him and the group of Young Lords with him in the middle of the sanctuary, leaving some with broken arms and legs.

Three weeks later the Young Lords broke in and took over the church building and renamed it The People's Church. They ran the breakfast program and day care, along with free clothing drives, political education classes, free health programs, and nightly entertainment for thousands of community members for eleven days until the police shut it down and arrested over one hundred Young Lord members and supporters.[5]

During those eleven days, the People's Church of the Young Lords did the work of caring for the community that the First Spanish United Methodist Church should have been doing all along. The church may have said yes to their calling, but they didn't follow it.

Who was obedient to God?

The Young Lords' mission was to care for their community the way they deserved to be cared for, and they knew they were following the teachings of Jesus more authentically than the leaders of that church. They said that if Christ were alive in their day, he would be a Young Lord.[6]

BIG CHURCH

I think back to Pope John Paul II sternly wagging his finger down at Ernesto Cardenal for helping liberate the Nicaraguan people and saying to Cardenal, "You must fix your affairs with the Church," and I feel like his perspective of "the church" was tragically small.

In 1310, the French Christian mystic Marguerite Porete was burned at the stake by Catholic Church authorities for heresy. She had written a book called *The Mirror of Simple Souls*, about achieving union with God through completely surrendering your will to the will of God. The problem for the Catholic Church was that this unification meant she had no need for the church to mediate between God and the human soul.

To the clergy's dismay, Porete made a sharp distinction between "Sainte Eglise la Petite" (Holy Church the Little) and "Sainte Eglise la Grande" (Holy Church the Great), or as John Caputo paraphrases it: "little c" church and "Big C" Church.[7] Typically we'd refer to a local congregation as the "little c" church and refer to the larger institution with all its laws, sacraments, and doctrines as the "Big C" Church. Porete inverted that and insisted that the *institution* was the little church, and the big Church was the work of love in the world, inspiring the institution.

Of course they killed her.

Porete was inspired by 1 John 4, which reads as pretty scandalous with these ideas in mind.

Beloved, let us love one another, because love is from God; everyone who loves is born of God and knows God. Whoever does not love does not know God, for God is love. God's love was revealed among us in this way: God sent his only Son into the world so that we might live through him. In this is love, not that we loved God but that he loved us and sent his Son to be the atoning sacrifice for our sins. Beloved, since God loved us so much, we also ought to love one another. No one has ever seen God; if we love one another, God lives in us, and his love is perfected in us.[8]

Everyone who loves knows God. Those who say they know God, but do not love, do not know God. Being governed by love transcends religious identity. Even the way that John speaks of "the Son" is fascinating. God is revealed as love through the Son, Jesus Christ. Even though love exists beyond the Christian story, the Christian story teaches that love is revealed to us particularly through the sacrifice of Jesus, but it doesn't stop there. After we experience this love particularly, we become capable of discovering love *universally*, now that we know what to look for. So, of course, we find this universal love in all kinds of unexpected places, beyond religious boundaries. That's the big Church, outdoing the little church in its institution.

Porete writes, "I am God, says Love, for Love is God and God is Love, and this Soul is God by the condition of Love."[9]

My friend Kyle told me about one of the first pickets he took a group of volunteers to where he experienced the power of solidarity on a visceral level with all his senses. The crowd chanted in unison, "*Thank you, we love you! Thank you, we love you! Thank you, we love you!*"

This is a common chant in activist circles shouted by a crowd as someone is released from jail for civil disobedience. "*Thank you, we love you!*" is chanted when someone is released after being arrested in an anti-war protest or a Black Lives Matter protest, or a worker strike. "*Thank you, we love you!*" is sometimes even chanted when someone joins a picket. Kyle's first time hearing this chant made him tear up and realize this was a new type of love he hadn't recognized before. And that love was working-class solidarity.

Thank you, we love you!

It's a common experience to go to a protest or a strike and feel something spiritual. Some even say it feels like church, except somehow it feels even more like church than actual church ever felt. Individual bodies join together to create one body fighting for justice for one another, and if you know what that feels like, then you know what the church is supposed to feel like.

The church is called to be the collective body of Christ. In 1 Corinthians 12, Paul says that if one member of the body suffers, we all suffer. The slogan for the Industrial Workers of the World is "an injury to one is an injury to all." This kind of solidarity cannot be contained by the little church in its institution.

The God of the big church—the God that is love—shows up in all the places you would least expect, including (perhaps especially) in places where we might have assumed there was a rejection of God. This shouldn't surprise us anymore. This God is bigger than that.

WHEN WE LOVE

On my last night leading the youth group as an evangelical youth pastor, I told the students that I felt like God was calling me elsewhere. I felt called to speak to a more *post-Christian* environment.

Because of my openness I had constantly found myself in conversations with Christians who would feel comfortable telling me things like, "I usually believe in all this stuff, but sometimes I doubt, and I don't know what to do with that." And I was able to tell those people, "That's okay. That's part of it. Explore that." Then eventually I noticed that my openness also led me to conversations with non-religious people who would feel comfortable telling me things like, "I usually doubt all this stuff, but sometimes I believe, and I don't know what to do with that." And I was able to tell those people, "That's okay. That's part of it. Explore that." So I told my youth group that I was becoming a lot more interested in those latter conversations.

Then I told them that after years of struggling with questions about God, the only thing I'm certain of is that God is revealed to the fullest when we love one another. I was paraphrasing 1 John 4:12, which says, "No one has ever seen God. But if we love each other, God lives in us, and his love is brought to full expression in us."

When you follow this love, life naturally leads you beyond limited conceptions of God, and you discover God in the most unexpected places. I wanted those students to remember that truth more than anything I had ever said to them. And that's probably why my pastor/boss didn't let me speak to the larger congregation when he announced my departure.

The Christianity of Christ has become so unfamiliar to those committed to the Christianity of this land that they cannot recognize the work of Christ being done outside of the institutional church. In fact, they actively fight against it.

When Jesus announced his mission to bring good news to the poor, proclaim release to the captives, restore sight to the blind, and to let the oppressed go free, I am certain he wasn't too concerned with that holy work of liberation being done under the banner of a specific religion. The mission was the work. The mission was not to get everyone to use the same name for the work.

Many of us who have left Christian communities continue this work, even if we stop using the same old names for it. And for many of us, giving up those old names is what enabled us to authentically commit ourselves to this work.

You have not gone astray. You have been on one long path. And this path leads us to discover God in more authentic ways than we ever could have by following the Christianity of this land. They cannot stop us from doing the holy work of liberation God calls us to.

8

A RIOT AT THE TEMPLE

For a couple of years I had to attend a prayer meeting before each Sunday morning service at a church I was serving in. I slowly began to dread it. Every week we prayed for people to have an experience with God that morning in the service, as if God were in the building and people were coming in from the godless world to meet with God. But every week I kept getting a creeping feeling that this framing was the opposite of the truth.

First, God does not live in the church building alone, and most of my peers would have agreed with that, but I also understood that people were actually coming in from a *God-soaked* world, and were bringing God into the church building as we gathered together. Praying those prayers inside that building every Sunday created a feeling of gnawing emptiness inside me. As I prayed, I heard a small voice within me saying, "God is not in here. God is outside." That voice grew louder and louder as the weeks went by, and I was only able to avoid an exhausting discomfort by walking outside and continuing to pray in the parking lot. Gradually, my prayers turned to cultivating an openness to an experience of God who was always coming from the outside world into the church to disrupt the familiar performances of Christian ministers.

What started as a scary feeling now seems like an obvious spiritual truth. As the apostle Paul said in Acts 17, God does not live in churches, temples, shrines, or any other religious buildings made by human hands.[1] In fact, the prophets throughout the Bible always come with a message of criticism, not for the world, but for the religious authorities in the temple or the church. When you are open to the experience of God within the world, then you discover the blasphemous smallness of the God bound up inside the walls of the church. And you start to resonate more and more with the religion of the prophets who always saved their sharpest criticisms for the church.

Jesus aligned himself with this prophetic tradition. The clearest example of this is the story of Jesus entering the temple, starting a riot, and preaching against the religious authorities. This was not a temper tantrum. This was a planned demonstration that communicated the justice Jesus wanted to see in the world. Jesus was not the first one to protest in the temple, and he wasn't the last. Jesus was part of a long prophetic stream of those who called for justice in the location where injustice had been justified again and again.

HOW THE WORLD CHANGES

Remember, the desire for a new world emerges as a solution to the problems of the current world. Those problems are first named by powerless people who experience the constraints of the current world. It is through their collective organizing and revolt that more and more people begin to comprehend the intolerability of the constraints of the current world. Revolt is a process, not a singular event.[2] No small instance of revolt proposes to be the solution to the problems of the current world. Rather, every small instance of revolt raises the consciousness of the masses to inspire unity in the process of revolt. Eventually, this process leads to the development of a new world. This is how historical change works. And God is always on the side of the powerless as they struggle for liberation and build a new world.

Building a new world begins with raising people's consciousness to the constraints experienced by the powerless of the current world. Protests, riots, and strikes have increased over the last few years as part of the same work, led by the powerless who have experienced the constraints of *this* world.

Jesus was also participating in this work through his ministry. This is most obvious in Jesus's actions in the temple. The riots of Black Lives Matter protests and the riot of Jesus in the temple are both doing something similar in their societies. By reading these riots side by side, we can gain a deeper understanding of each of them and begin to discover their historical significance.

WHAT IS UPSURGING FROM BELOW?

The process that leads to the development of a new world begins by listening to what is being communicated in these forms of protest. We must listen to those who experience the constraints of the current world in order to understand how to build a new world.

Many people have gone to Black Lives Matter protests and are quick to claim that the most aggressive protesters are making the protest into something that it wasn't supposed to be about. The wise ones are willing to stop and ask themselves *Am I the one who is actually wrong about what this protest is about?* We are quick to assume the naivete of others before ever exposing it in ourselves. Many people went to a protest in the summer of 2020 expecting to protest the arrest of police officer Derek Chauvin, and then were surprised to discover the general anti-police sentiment of many protests.

"A riot is the language of the unheard," people repeated to each other amid the frustration, quoting an old Dr. King interview, while trying to satisfy their own complex feelings. Many people were fine with a couple of days of protests, hoping it would lead to an increase in the police budget, so they could get some better training. The protests, however, just wouldn't stop.

The media sensationalized every tiny moment of property destruction, vandalism, and looting because that's what gets attention as networks compete with one another for clicks and ratings. This made it seem like every moment of every protest was a destructive riot. By doing this, they manufactured a new narrative that left them with only two choices: either support *all* forms of violence and destruction from every side, or give your sole support to the "peaceful," "nonviolent" protests of those fighting for reform alone. The ones who wanted more than reform were painted as violent extremists who must be condemned "if you really cared about Black lives and really wanted to make some realistic changes."

This narrative exposes the obvious tactic here: the refusal to listen. It's a refusal to listen to the message of the protest and a manipulation of the message by creating a narrative of a "real reason" for protesting while condemning the reasons of all the others as violent extremism.

This gave the perfect opportunity for all the white moderates to say, "Of course I believe Black Lives

Matter, I just don't support (insert whatever was demonized by the media that day)." This isn't that different from the white moderate spoken of by Dr. King,

who is more devoted to "order" than to justice; who prefers a negative peace which is the absence of tension to a positive peace which is the presence of justice; who constantly says: "I agree with you in the goal you seek, but I cannot agree with your methods of direct action..."[3]

The subtle, unspoken message I sense from the white moderate of today is: "I believe Black lives matter, but I don't want to eliminate the institutions that were built, and are continually funded, to destroy Black lives."

So let's begin listening to the entire protest, including the parts that make us uncomfortable. Let's listen to the larger spirit of revolt that each of these protests live within.

Marxist humanist philosopher Raya Dunayevskaya, while discussing the revolutionary movements around the world throughout the twentieth century, reminds us to take notice of "certain creative moments in history" when "the self-determination of ideas and the self-determination of masses readying for revolt explode."

These are the moments where we must pay attention with, as Jesus said, eyes to see and ears to hear. "Something is in the air, and you catch it," Dunayevskaya explains. "That is, you catch it if you have a clear head and if you have good ears to hear what is upsurging from below."[4]

The protest, and often the riot, is an expression of what is upsurging from below. When we claim that the protests are supposed to be only about this or that, we are refusing to listen, and are contributing to the historic suppression of what is upsurging from below.

Jesus led a few disruptive demonstrations that also tapped into what was upsurging from below, beginning with riding into Jerusalem on something as lowly as a donkey. Now celebrated by Christians on the first day of Holy Week as Palm Sunday, stripped away from its political context, this demonstration harbored a dangerous message that would lead to Jesus's public execution by the end of the week. The way Jesus entered Jerusalem at the beginning of Passover week was a strategically organized demonstration.

Jesus's entire ministry was headed toward Jerusalem. Every time he had to leave a large crowd of sick people begging to be healed, it was because his journey was aimed toward Jerusalem. Word of Jesus's message had already spread to Jews in Jerusalem, and they were prepared to participate in these planned demonstrations. Mark 11 tells us that when Jesus and his disciples were approaching Jerusalem, he told two of his disciples, "Go into the village ahead of you, and immediately as you enter it, you will find tied there a colt that has never been ridden; untie it and bring it. If anyone says to you, 'Why are you doing this?' just say this, 'The Lord needs it and will send it back here immediately.'"[5]

We don't know who was assigned to tie up the colt at the entrance, but taking the colt communicated to the crowds waiting in Jerusalem that Jesus was about to arrive. From the Mount of Olives, Jesus entered through the east entrance of Jerusalem on the colt while a crowd surrounded him, preparing the road for Jesus by spreading their cloaks and "leafy branches that they had cut in the fields" on the ground. And they shouted, "Hosanna! Blessed is the one who comes in the name of the Lord! Blessed is the coming kingdom of our ancestor David! Hosanna in the highest heaven!"[6]

This deliberate sequence of actions was a symbolic reenactment of the prophecy of Zechariah. Zechariah 9:9 says, "Rejoice greatly, O daughter Zion! Shout aloud, O daughter Jerusalem! Lo, your king comes to you; triumphant and victorious is he, humble and riding on a donkey, on a colt, the foal of a donkey." Matthew even directly quotes the verse in his account.

This was a purposefully timed demonstration that would also remind people of the next verse in Zechariah 9: "He will cut off the chariot from Ephraim and the war-horse from Jerusalem; and the battle bow shall be cut off, and he shall command peace to the nations; his dominion shall be from sea to sea, and from the River to the ends of the earth."

Although the gospel accounts do not report this detail, we know that the Roman governor Pontius Pilate arrived in Jerusalem at the beginning of Passover Week as well. First-century Jewish historian Josephus wrote that during every Passover, Pontius Pilate and a legion of Roman soldiers spent the week in Jerusalem because of an increased chance of an uprising as Jews celebrated the event of the Exodus. The Romans wanted to make sure nobody got any dangerous ideas as they recounted God's attack on Egypt and the liberation of the Israelites.[7]

So as Jesus humbly entered Jerusalem from the east on a donkey, surrounded by a crowd of peasants and leafy branches, Pontius Pilate was likely entering Jerusalem from the west on a chariot led by a war horse, surrounded by a legion of Roman soldiers with armor and deadly weaponry. In their book on Jesus's last week in Jerusalem, John Dominic Crossan and Marcus Borg point out, "What we often call Jesus's triumphal entry was actually an anti-imperial, anti-triumphal one, a deliberate lampoon of the conquering emperor entering a city on horseback through gates opened in abject submission."[8]

The symbolism is packed with meaning for the lives of those in the crowd surrounding Jesus. This demonstration exposed two warring kingdoms: the kingdom of Rome, with the power and weapons on their side, and the kingdom of God with the people on their side, desperate for liberation.

At the end of the day, Jesus and his disciples discreetly traveled back through the Mount of Olives to Bethany, where they stayed every night that week, likely to avoid arrest in Jerusalem after sundown with no crowds around to protect Jesus. The next day Jesus and his disciples traveled back to Jerusalem for another demonstration, this time at the temple. Mark says,

> Then they came to Jerusalem. And he entered the temple and began to drive out those who were selling and those who were buying in the temple, and he overturned the tables of the money changers and the seats of those who sold doves; and he would not allow anyone to carry anything through the temple.[9]

It's important to notice that Jesus's actions are not random here. They are calculated. He is not throwing a tantrum, spontaneously triggered by witnessing something uniquely scandalous happening in the temple. Jesus isn't just knocking over whatever is in his way. When we look at his specific actions, we notice that Jesus drove out those who were buying and selling, overturned the money changers' tables, and overturned the seats of those who sold doves. Jesus is staging a temporary shutdown of the temple's activities to get the attention of those present.

Jesus's shutdown of the temple was his second demonstration that week, and the one that would lead to his arrest and execution just a couple of days later. Jesus avoids arrest this day by being protected by the large crowds, and he ends the day by sneaking back to Bethany for the night. Eventually, this nightly passage through the Mount of Olives would be exposed, leading to his arrest.

THE RIOT AS A REJECTION OF THE CURRENT WORLD

It's important to notice the lack of a spirit of reform in these demonstrations. The spirit of abolition is the driving force here. What is being communicated in these demonstrations is a rejection of the current world, not its reform.

On May 28, 2020, the third night of protests in Minneapolis after the police murder of George Floyd, protesters set the Minneapolis Police Department's Third Precinct building on fire. The precinct was where the four officers involved in the murder were based, so protesters had been gathered around the building since the first night.

Some thought the fire was taking things too far. Most of these people, however, seemed to view the act strictly as a response to the murder of George Floyd. Those who viewed the fire as a response to centuries of racist violence experienced a kind of catharsis witnessing a police precinct in flames. The last time a police station had been destroyed in the United States was in 1863 during the New York draft riots.

Queen Jacobs, a Minneapolis swim instructor, arrived at the scene after the fire had begun. "I think we all felt a sense of strength and community, and a piece of what our ancestors went through, and when they were able to be liberated," she said. "We're done backing down. We're done rolling over. We're done dying."[10]

For the crime of conspiracy to commit arson, the police arrested and charged two white men, Dylan Shakespeare Robinson and Branden Michael Wolfe, along with two Black men, Davon De-Andre Turner and Bryce Michael Williams. Although many more participated in setting the station on fire, these four men were the ones caught on the video that was posted to social media.

In an Instagram interview shortly after that night, Bryce Williams said, "For once we feel like we're in complete control. The police can't do anything. We're burning down their sanctuary, their home."[11]

Juno Choi, the owner of a local brewery a few doors down from the precinct, said, "It has become sort of symbolic of police brutality and systemic racism across the country. It was really a protest about what's been going on all across the nation for a long, long time."[12]

Jennifer Starr Dodd, a relief emergency organizer for the local Holy Trinity Lutheran Church, said, "I think of it as the Pentecost." Pentecost refers to the story in Acts 2 when the Holy Spirit appeared to Jesus's disciples through a rushing wind and "tongues of fire." "It's like a holy anger," Dodd said. "The spirit came and it was a great fire, and everybody changed in that moment of Pentecost. I see the burning of the Third Precinct as the same. It changed everyone, whether they like it or not."[13]

That night I watched the fire on a livestream, and I was overwhelmed with similar feelings as I saw hundreds of people cheering and dancing in front of the flames. When shutdowns began in response to the spread of the deadly coronavirus, many people asked, "Where is God in all this?" Since this question was at the front of my mind during this season, I couldn't help but think: there, among those celebrating in front of that burning police station is exactly where God is to be found. And I couldn't help but think of Jesus, who rioted in the temple two thousand years ago.

It's important we understand exactly what Jesus was protesting in the temple when he shut down its activities. To assume that Jesus's demonstration in the temple was protesting the temple itself would be a misinterpretation. It would also be a misinterpretation to assume that Jesus was protesting the sacrificial system housed at the temple, or even worse, to assume that Jesus was protesting Judaism.

To help us understand what Jesus was protesting, let's look at a scene in Mark right before Jesus's temple demonstration. That morning on the way to Jerusalem, Jesus looked for something to eat.

Seeing in the distance a fig tree in leaf, he went to see whether perhaps he would find anything on it. When he came to it, he found nothing but leaves, for it was not the season for figs. He said to it, "May no one ever eat fruit from you again." And his disciples heard it.[14]

Jesus enters the temple in the very next verse. It's clear that Jesus's cursing of the fig tree is a symbol for how Jesus approaches the temple. As Borg and Crossan point out, "In both cases, the problem is a lack of the 'fruit' that Jesus expected to be present."[15]

A DEN OF ROBBERS

After Jesus shut down the activities in the temple, he began teaching, saying, "Is it not written, 'My house shall be called a house of prayer for all the nations'? But you have made it a den of robbers."[16] Some have made the mistake of interpreting the reference to a den of robbers as Jesus claiming that people are being robbed in the temple, literally or symbolically. However, a den of robbers is not a place where robbers steal. A den of robbers is where robbers run and hide, expecting to be safe.

In the same way that Jesus was reenacting Zechariah's prophecy while riding the donkey into Jerusalem, Jesus is reenacting an earlier Hebrew prophet's demonstration in the temple. The Jewish crowds would have been certain of this connection the moment Jesus said the temple had been made into a den of robbers, directly quoting Jeremiah. Roughly six hundred years before

Jesus's temple demonstration, the prophet Jeremiah spoke at the gate of the temple,

> Thus says the Lord of hosts, the God of Israel: Amend your ways and your doings, and let me dwell with you in this place. Do not trust in these deceptive words: "This is the temple of the Lord, the temple of the Lord, the temple of the Lord."[17]

Jeremiah seems prepared for the accusation of blasphemy as he condemns those in the temple. The ritualistic way of proclaiming the temple of the Lord as indeed the holy and glorious cannot save people from the correction Jeremiah is about to deliver. Jeremiah begins by naming the deceptive nature of the claim that the temple of the Lord is the wrong place to speak his message. It is in the place where people thought they could hide in safety that they needed to hear this condemnation. Jeremiah continues, speaking on behalf of God:

> For if you truly amend your ways and your doings, if you truly act justly one with another, if you do not oppress the alien, the orphan, and the widow, or shed innocent blood in this place, and if you do not go after other gods to your own hurt, then I will dwell with you in this place, in the land that I gave of old to your ancestors forever and ever. Here you are, trusting in deceptive words to no avail. Will you steal, murder, commit adultery, swear falsely, make offerings to Baal, and go after other gods that you have not known, and then come and stand before me in this house, which is called by my name, and say,

"We are safe!"—only to go on doing all these abominations? Has this house, which is called by my name, become a den of robbers in your sight? You know, I too am watching, says the Lord.[18]

In December 2014, during Christmas shopping season, more than one thousand protesters filled the Mall of America in Minneapolis in response to the police murders of Michael Brown and Eric Garner. Twenty-five people were arrested for trespassing. Exactly one year later, organizers planned to protest in the mall again in response to the Minneapolis Police murder of Jamar Clark. The day before the protest, CNN's Carol Costello interviewed the attorney of the Mall of America, who said they "totally respect the message" and "totally respect their free speech rights," but "a demonstration doesn't belong on private property." She added, "Come here and shop. School choirs come and sing holiday music. That is what we're about. We're not about demonstrations."[19]

Then Costello brought on Black Lives Matter organizer Miski Noor. Costello pressured, "Why not just move your protest outside? People can see you're protesting as they pull into the parliament by the parking lot by the thousands. What's wrong with that?" Noor responded,

Carol, it also brings to mind the idea . . . that Dr. King said, about people who agree with your message but not with your tactics.

We don't need anybody to agree with our tactics, right? We're disrupting business as usual. That is the whole idea. We're not going to stand in a corner and protest, because nobody pays attention to that. We are going disrupt your life. You are going to know that business as usual in America and the world is not going to continue while black people–unarmed black people–are literally being shot and killed by law enforcement in the street every day.[20]

Before being dismissed, Noor also made sure to shed light on the ways the Mall of America participates in "anti-Black racism and white supremacy":

The Mall of America has been investigated by the Minnesota Department of Human Rights for violations for the way they treat people of color in the mall. So these same issues that we're seeing in police departments are manifesting in the mall, and people of color and black people are being affected negatively because of the way the mall decides to act. So that is why they are an appropriate target.[21]

It is an ancient tactic to shut down protest by claiming the place people choose to protest is the wrong place and the wrong time. And yet, the places where people think they can avoid confronting their injustice are often the best places to confront it. The Mall of America is this type of place. The Minneapolis Third Precinct is this type of place. And the temple is this type of place.

MAKING THE CURRENT WORLD INTOLERABLE

Requiring peaceful protests that don't disrupt any-thing—or be met with police violence—exposes that the United States has always suppressed the free speech of protesters. Those who claim to "support the message" but not protesters' disruptive tactics are disguising their real desire: to not be inconvenienced or challenged by protesters at all.

There must be a disruption of everyday life in order to make a change. Many people did not realize how much of a problem police violence was until the pro-tests went on a couple of days longer than expected. When that happens, people are forced to listen in ways they couldn't have before.

There are many in this country whose lives are intol-erable, and in order to bring attention to their struggle they must make others experience a glimpse of intoler-ability. When that happens, people are exposed to all the ways we tolerate the intolerable every day. We gain "eyes to see" and "ears to hear" through the aggressive experience of being exposed to what we can no longer unsee and unhear.

Jesus's demonstration exposed people to the ways they tolerated the intolerable as well. Jesus chose to dis-rupt the temple during Passover week, the busiest time of the year. I imagine there were those back then who "supported Jesus's message" but didn't think the temple during Passover was the right place and time to protest.

We would call a person naive, if not deceptive, if they were to tell Jesus that he should have demonstrated in some other public area during some other time. We should think that response to Black Lives Matter protests is just as naive, if not deceptive.

In Matthew's account, the author mostly copies Mark. After Jesus calls the temple a den of robbers, Matthew adds in verse 14:

> The blind and the lame came to him in the temple, and he cured them. But when the chief priests and the scribes saw the amazing things that he did, and heard the children crying out in the temple, "Hosanna to the Son of David," they became angry and said to him, "Do you hear what these are saying?" Jesus said to them, "Yes; have you never read, 'Out of the mouths of infants and nursing babies you have prepared praise for yourself'?"[22]

It's beautiful and inspiring to imagine this scene of a crowd of disabled people rushing into the temple. Jesus once again crosses social boundaries as he makes the temple his center for healing those who had been cast out again and again. In the temple that had taken so much wealth in tithes and taxes, Jesus illuminates those who had suffered the most from a lack of wealth and resources. Jesus once again demonstrates what the upside-down reign of God looks like, where the last become first.

Jesus tapped into the Hebrew prophetic tradition and spoke against the injustice happening, not in the temple, but everywhere, and he condemned those who treat the temple as a safe refuge in which to hide from the consequences of their unjust actions.

We need to place Jesus's antagonism toward the temple in its proper context. An adequate comparison is the way Frederick Douglass talked about the Christianity of Christ vs. the Christianity of the land, the religion of the slaveholders. In the name of the Christianity of Christ, Douglass condemned and rejected the Christianity of the land. Similarly, within Jewish history the Hebrew prophets condemned and rejected the Judaism of the land in the name of the prophetic Judaism of justice. The Judaism often critiqued by the prophets was one that had prioritized worship over justice. Jesus continues the tradition of the Hebrew prophets in the temple.

The temple was also the socioeconomic center that symbolized the collaboration between the Jewish priesthood and the Roman government. The temple had been tainted by compromise since the Jews were conquered by the Persian empire in the sixth century BCE. While the Babylonians had previously destroyed the first temple and deported the Jews, the Persians allowed the priesthood to rebuild the temple, but created a double role for the priesthood to also serve as officers of the Persian emperor. The emperor saw the compromise as conveniently practical, requiring the Jews to pay their taxes to the Persian government along with their tithes to the priests.[23] From the Persians to the Greeks to the Romans, the priests profited from this collaboration and used the Torah to justify their privileged social position while preaching pacifism to the peasants whose poverty continued to grow more and more unbearable.[24]

During Jesus's day, under the Roman Empire, people were required to make sacrifices to Caesar as Lord in the temple as well. Herod the Great had renovated the temple around 20 BCE and built a portico above it where soldiers would stand guard when there was an increased chance of an uprising, such as Passover week. When discussing whether the people supported the temple, we must distinguish between the temple as a symbol of Jewish faith and the actual temple system that had been compromised by the Roman government.[25]

If Jesus wanted to protest Judaism, or the sacrificial system specifically, then he could have easily overturned items inside the temple where sacrifices were taking place. Instead, Jesus shut down the temple in the outer courts where people were buying and selling. As Horsley puts it, "Jesus attacks the activities in which the exploitation of God's people by their priestly rulers was most visible."[26]

The Gospel of Luke adds a scene right before Jesus enters the temple:

> As he came near and saw the city, he wept over it, saying, "If you, even you, had only recognized on this day the things that make for peace! But now they are hidden from your eyes.

Indeed, the days will come upon you, when your enemies will set up ramparts around you and surround you, and hem you in on every side. They will crush you to the ground, you and your children within you, and they will not leave within you one stone upon another; because you did not recognize the time of your visitation from God."[27]

The original readers of this gospel would have understood this passage as a reference to the destruction of the temple in 70 CE, which was the Roman response to a Jewish revolt in 66 CE against the Roman Empire. Mark was the first gospel written, around 70 CE, while Matthew, Luke, and John were written during the following decades. An earlier Jewish revolt took place in 4 BCE, which was also brutally crushed by Rome. Jesus's ministry took place between these two revolts, but the gospels were written down after the temple was destroyed in 70 CE.

Jesus either predicted the destruction of the temple or Luke retroactively placed these words on the lips of Jesus as a way of letting his audience know that Jesus's actions are part of the larger sequence of events that would lead to the destruction of the temple. Either way it's safe to assume that the historical Jesus truly did see the end of the temple as inevitable. Even Jeremiah had a similar outlook of the temple. Jeremiah, Jesus, and other prophets witnessed the people of their day prioritize worship over justice and understood that this path would only lead to the destruction of the places in which they worship.

We gain a wider perspective of the ministry of Jesus when we learn that it took place between these two major violent Jewish revolts in 4 BCE and 66 CE, both of which resulted in massive Roman suppression. Jesus and his followers did not condemn these revolts. They easily could have, but they did not. They understood that they were a part of an inevitable stream of conflict that rages on before a new world is birthed, as do many people who protest and revolt against the current world.

Jesus did not advocate for violence, but we must also recognize that Jesus did not advocate for nonviolence either. In fact, he believed God would violently destroy the Roman Empire, like many Jews of his time did. What Jesus was more interested in was showing people a new way to live in preparation for the new world that would be birthed from the destruction of the Roman Empire.

Jesus advocated for a way of communal life committed to sacrificial love and the liberation of the oppressed. By teaching the values of a new world, Jesus and his followers raised the consciousness of people who couldn't imagine what life would look like beyond the current world.

THE RIOT AS A BIRTH OF A NEW WORLD

Remember, the type of rejection of the current world that we're talking about has nothing to do with an obsession with destruction or death. Protesting the current world is driven by the desire for a new world. Working toward the development of a new world is the sole reason for rejecting the current world here.

In her book, *In Defense of Looting*, historian Vicky Osterweil talks about historical movements that were birthed out of historical riots. Osterweil reminds us that the "Stonewall riots gave birth to the gay liberation movement; the storming of the Bastille gave birth to the French Revolution; the Boston Tea Party, the American Revolution."[28]

She also reminds us that the physical birth of a child can be violent and dangerous, even "life-threatening," so we should expect the same of the births that are achieved through riots.

> Riots are violent, extreme, and femme as fuck: they rip, tear, burn, and destroy to give birth to a new world. They can emerge from rising tensions and lead to nothing—a miscarriage—or be the height and end point of a given movement. In most instances, however, they transform and build a nascent moment into a movement: rioting, as the Black trans women of Stonewall showed us, is a form of queer birth.[29]

We must pay attention to what riots are struggling to give birth to. Those who are fighting solely for reform often believe they are the only ones concerned with a new world, dismissing abolitionists as people who are obsessed with tearing everything down. That's one of the common arguments used to shut down ambitious conversations about alternatives to the prison–industrial complex.

Abolition, as Mariame Kaba says, "is a vision of a restructured society in a world where we have everything we need: food, shelter, education, health, art, beauty, clean water, and more things that are foundational to our personal and community safety."[30]

PIC abolitionists are committed to collectively solving socioeconomic problems that lead to crime. Police and prisons do not prevent crime. They only punish crime. The core motivation of abolition is building a new world, not tearing everything down. The thing is, at some point the current world must die for a new world to be birthed. That is how change happens.

After Jesus's demonstration at the temple, the Gospel of Mark again mentions the fig tree that Jesus had cursed the previous morning:

> In the morning as they passed by, they saw the fig tree withered away to its roots. Then Peter remembered and said to him, "Rabbi, look! The fig tree that you cursed has withered." Jesus answered them, "Have faith in God. Truly I tell you, if you say to this mountain, 'Be taken up and thrown into the sea,' and if you do not doubt in your heart, but believe that what you say will come to pass, it will be done for you. So I tell you, whatever you ask for in prayer, believe that you have received it, and it will be yours."[31]

When Jesus is walking through the Mount of Olives and says, "*This* mountain," in the distance they would have seen the Herodium, which may be the mountain Jesus was referring to. The Herodium was named by Herod the Great after himself, with an innovative palace-fortress built on top to celebrate his victory over the Hasmoneans and the Parthians in 40 BCE. Josephus described the mountain being artificially raised "by the hand of man and rounded off in the shape of a breast."[32] In honor of Herod the Great's military victory, the mountain was raised by enslaved workers who carried over pieces of another mountain from a nearby demolished hill. Herod the Great literally moved a mountain using enslaved people. Jesus may have been referring to Herod's ability to move mountains when he told his disciples that they can move mountains too.

We can make real transformation here and now. We don't have to prolong transformation to some sort of afterlife. Christians are called to materialize the reign of God on earth "as it is in heaven." In the reign of God, we—not just Herod—can move mountains. In the reign of God, the power dynamic is flipped upside down. In the reign of God, transformation comes from below, not above.

But not every single riot is attempting to give birth to a new world. Sometimes a riot emerges as to suppress the birth of a new world, in reaction to radical change. This is why the Capitol riot on January 6, 2021, does not fit into the kind of riots I'm talking about. Trump supporters stormed the Capitol building in protest of the alleged rigged presidential election of Joe Biden. And yet, it was about more than that.

Many of these protesters claimed that they were also taking the country back from an imagined cabal of elites that had led the country away from the traditional Christian nationalism of the past. Just as the slogan "Make America Great Again" implies, these protesters were not calling for anything new, but were calling for a violent suppression of those fighting for a new world. They were fighting for a cultural reversal to an old, imagined social order in which the "right people" were in charge.

Although the media portrayed this riot as an insurrection, this riot was more of an intimidation tactic. It was an attempt to show the world that they can cause disorder just like those who are fighting for a new world. It was an attempt to intimidate those who support the kind of revolt I've been talking about.

Building a new world will always be met with suppression. Those who contribute to that suppression believe that they are protecting what God has made and become ignorant of the new thing God is doing. Like Peter in Acts 10, they refuse to listen to God because of their previous experience of God.

Jesus is executed because fighting for a new world will always be met with suppression by those who benefit from the current world. Jesus is not on the side of those who fight to preserve the current world. Those people killed Jesus. Jesus is on the side of those who fight for a new world. Jesus sacrificed his life in that temple to prove that.

9

JESUS, THE OUTSIDE AGITATOR

I visited a Unitarian Universalist church for the first time in 2013. One of the first people I met there was a Christian. He said he joined the church because he grew tired of his old Lutheran church always talking about the death of Jesus. And at his new church they talked about the *life* of Jesus. I was also searching for a community that emphasized the life of Jesus.

Constant discussion of the death of Jesus often leaves people unsure about what to do with their lives. I grew up being told that Jesus died on the cross as God's punishment for our sins so that we may go to heaven. That's neat if I'm looking for a ticket to go somewhere nice after I die. It doesn't tell me much about how to live my life. Christians often told me we are called to spend our lives persuading other people to get that ticket to the good place, but that doesn't seem to be the life Jesus called people to.

Jesus doesn't call people to escape this world, but to transform it. His death on the cross is a consequence to living a life devoted to radical transformation. This transformation within the reign of God was a direct challenge to the ruling authorities of his day. Jesus was executed on the cross, as were all crucifixion victims, for the crime of sedition. "King of the Jews" was written on the cross above Jesus's head because his crime was claiming there was any other king but Caesar. He was executed in public on a hill, so everyone could see what happens to those who challenge the rule of Rome.

This is why it can be a little tricky to refer to Jesus as "innocent," as Christians often do when telling the story of the crucifixion. Jesus caused a destructive riot in the temple, threatened the destruction of the temple, and preached the reign of God—all seditious acts in the reign of Rome.

We tend to call Jesus innocent because we have an understanding that the laws Jesus broke were unjust. When looking at someone we admire, like Jesus, in a distant environment, it is easy to determine his innocence. We are not burdened with the respect for first-century Roman law. Without this burden we are capable of recognizing the difference between crime and harm. Not every crime is harmful. And not every harmful act is a crime. From a distance we can clearly recognize this distinction. Jesus's crimes were not harmful. The harm came from the Roman state that crucified people. But, of course, crucifixion was not a crime. State violence hardly ever is. Protesting state violence, however, no matter how unharmful, is always framed as immoral when interpreted through the lens of crime.

When we commit the crime of protesting the harm of state violence, we must make this distinction. If we make the mistake of seeing everything through the lens of crime, then we end up condemning protests for not fitting within the boundaries that the state requires. Seeing everything through the lens of harm allows us to properly protest harm.

A DISRUPTION OF EVERYTHING

Fighting for a new world is always a disruption of the current world. In fact, the values of the new world necessarily function as a disruption of the values of the current world. This is why protests often lead to property damage and looting. As people unite for the values of a new world, the values of the current world—such as protecting private property—become exposed as one of the tools that suppress the development of a new world.

The property damage that occurs during an uprising is always popularly perceived as morally wrong by the values of the current world because we see it through the lens of crime. Then, in the new world, people struggle to comprehend how people of the old world were so offended by the occasional moments of property damage that occurred during the necessary protests against harm. This is why we struggle to condone the property damage that occasionally occurs during Black Lives Matter demonstrations, but don't have any problem with Jesus's property damage in the temple.

In an interview with Ill Will, Richard Gilman-Opalsky said,

> We have to consider what happens to people, and especially to young people, when they participate in a revolt ... Nobody thinks they will end racism by burning a cop car. But people are changed by the experience of revolt. Listen to what they say. They are fed up and fighting back. They are experimenting with their own powers, their creative capabilities to fight the reality that threatens them. These existential, cultural, psychic, historic, and political experiences are not nothing. They may end up being everything in the long run.[1]

One of the ways people commonly disrupt the current world is by challenging the way we frame property. One of the easiest crimes to condemn during times of sustained protest is looting, which tends to happen as protests escalate. Cases of looting are often sensationalized in the mainstream media. The common narrative is that looters don't care about the reasons behind the protest and that they use the protest as an excuse to steal expensive items for themselves. When you look deeper at the nature of looting, however, that's not what we see. In *In Defense of Looting*, Vicky Osterweil says, "When something is looted, that thing's nature as a commodity is destroyed by its being taken for free, out of the cycle of exchange and profit. Everything in the store goes from being a commodity to becoming a gift."[2]

The motivation at the heart of looting is more about sharing than it is stealing, which is why we often see looting lead to piles of goods thrown into the street, free for everyone to take. That sharing of wealth "points to the collapse of the system by which the looted things produce value," Osterweil says. When people are condemned for looting, it is not just because they broke the law. They are condemned because looting "points to and immediately enacts a different relationship to property."[3]

Jesus's disruptive actions in the temple also enact a different relationship to property. We especially notice this in the Gospel of John's account of the event:

> In the temple he found people selling cattle, sheep, and doves, and the money changers seated at their tables. Making a whip of cords, he drove all of them out of the temple, both the sheep and the cattle. He also poured out the coins of the money changers and overturned their tables. He told those who were selling the doves, "Take these things out of here! Stop making my Father's house a marketplace!"[4]

Most people imagine Jesus with his whip of cords when they imagine this scene. That detail comes from John. Another detail John adds is that Jesus uses the whip to drive out not only the buyers and sellers but also their products: the sheep and cattle. John also uniquely depicts Jesus pouring out the coins of the money changers. Jesus is literally looting here. Looting doesn't always mean keeping looted items. It simply means removing them from "the cycle of exchange and profit." Jesus loots the animals being bought and sold and loots the money too. He then accuses them of making the temple a "marketplace." The temple was supposed to be dedicated to the God who had liberated the Jews from slavery, but it had become complicit in another form of slavery that the Jews found themselves in under the Roman Empire: the slavery of debt.

Jesus also destroys property when he flips the tables, which were likely fragile and destroyed when flipped. Jesus's demonstration, like many demonstrations, led to property destruction and looting. Some may want to refute this comparison and argue that the difference is that Jesus didn't destroy property and loot just for the sake of destroying property and looting. Here's the thing though: Modern-day protesters don't either. Jesus and modern-day protesters participated in this kind of riotous behavior to send a message that was being suppressed.

OUTSIDE AGITATORS

Many people dismiss property destruction and looting by claiming that it's led by "outside agitators," and not by the "real" protesters who "really" care. Osterweil calls this caricature "a white supremacist classic, going all the way back to slavery."

Under slavery, Osterweil says, plantation owners blamed "scheming Northerners" for stirring up their enslaved workers, deluding them with "ideas of freedom and equality." The racist assumption at the root of this claim "forms the logic behind the 'outside agitator.'" The phrase emerged during the Civil Rights era and continues to be used today, along with its various contemporary forms, such as "white anarchists," "antifa," "agent provocateurs," or the fictional "George Soros–funded career activists." Osterweil sharply challenges the assumptions that any of these groups is responsible for stirring protesters up:

> This logic strips those who protest of their power, claiming that their experiences, lives, and desires are not actually sufficient to inspire their acts of resistance—implying that they don't know what they're doing. It also begins from the presumption that the world is fine as it is, and so only nihilistic or paid troublemakers could challenge it. But it is a racist idea on its face. What actually is wrong with an outside agitator?[5]

Jesus's critics could have easily labeled him an outside agitator as well. Coming from a poor town in Galilee, Jesus riots in the temple, causing trouble and stirring up others. His arrest and execution were inevitable.

Protesting oppressive institutions in a way that has an impact will always have deadly consequences. This is the risk taken by all who participate in this process.

Fighting for this new world is the most honorable cause in the eyes of those in the new world, and the most dishonorable cause in the eyes of those in the current world. Those who fight to preserve this world as it is are idolized. Those who fight for a new world are vilified.

Many will condemn a protest as illegitimate when protesters break the law or resist arrest. But it is nonsensical to require those protesting the unjust law to follow the unjust law they are protesting. The law is a representation of the state's monopoly on violence. The law permits state forces to enact violence by any means necessary to protect the law, so their actions are not popularly perceived as violent since they are not technically "breaking the law." All forms of counterviolence, even counterviolence through property damage, are popularly perceived as wrong because of the law that was designed to suppress their resistance.

Of course, there will always be parts of different protests that we condemn because we do not always act in our best interests. However, the actions of protesters that we condemn should be observed through the lens of harm, not through the lens of crime. Determining harm and determining whether some harm is ever morally justifiable should be discussed, but that determination should not be made through the lens of crime, since the interpretation of crime depends on who holds the monopoly on violence. Condemning protests through the lens of crime obscures the harm that people are protesting, perpetuating the lie that protesters who break the law are just as bad as those they're protesting against.

Jesus broke the law, but we proclaim him innocent because he did not cause harm. Let's keep that same energy with everyone else.

PICK UP YOUR CROSS

It's clear Jesus knew he would be arrested and executed, as he and his disciples snuck back and forth through the Mount of Olives to stay in Bethany at night. Jesus was finally arrested in the Mount of Olives when his disciples, who were supposed to keep watch while he prayed, fell asleep. Jesus knew his resistance would lead to his execution, and his disciples knew they were risking their own lives as well.

A common saying of the Christian life since the early church is "Pick up your cross and follow me." This saying has been interpreted alongside other New Testament passages that speak about *rejoicing* in suffering. Unfortunately, many have interpreted this idea as a command for passivity in the face of oppression. Oppressors teach the oppressed to "rejoice in suffering" and passively accept their abuse with gratitude.

However, the New Testament's idea of rejoicing in suffering had nothing to do with passivity. Firstly, the suffering being referred to is the violent suppression from the powerful when you commit to a life of liberation. The apostle Paul tells Christians to rejoice in their suffering because of the larger process of justice that is enacted in the world through those who are willing to struggle for the cause of liberation. A life of passivity would be one that avoids resistance and is safe from potential suppression. Taking up your cross and rejoicing in suffering is about accepting that you will suffer more than others because you choose a life of resistance to injustice, and not a life of passivity that may warrant less suffering.

FATHER, FORGIVE THEM

In Luke 23, Jesus says on the cross, "Father, forgive them; for they do not know what they are doing."[6] This is the only instance in Jesus's ministry where he forgives someone who isn't in a marginalized position in society, and he gives it to the soldiers who kill him. Jesus always forgives those who are the most dehumanized by society, and before he dies, he forgives these soldiers who are also dehumanized—albeit in a much different way—by the Roman power structure.

In *Pedagogy of the Oppressed*, Paulo Freire explains how oppressors gradually dehumanize themselves the longer they dehumanize others. The oppressed must struggle for their own freedom and dignity as they restore their humanity by abolishing the systems that sustain their oppression. However, another important part of this process is the oppressed restoring the humanity of their oppressors too by taking "away oppressors' power to dominate and suppress." Freire argues, "It is only the oppressed who, by freeing themselves, can free their oppressors. The latter, as an oppressive class, can free neither others nor themselves."[7]

Taking away the ability to oppress from those in positions of oppressive power is difficult, because to the oppressor, taking away their power feels like a form of oppression. They won't have the ability to understand how oppressive their role in society is until their ability to oppress is taken away. Just as Jesus said, "they do not know what they are doing," because by dehumanizing others they have dehumanized themselves to the extent that they can't comprehend the impact of their actions. We can never expect our oppression to end by the hand of those in positions of power. We cannot persuade them to see the error of their ways. The only way they can understand the impact of their actions is through the oppressed taking away their power.

Authentic transformation can come only from below, not above. Only those who experience the constraints of the current world can figure out how to build a better world and then build it. Those who significantly benefit from the power and privilege they hold in the current world cannot lead the transformation our world desperately needs because they "do not know what they are doing."

Jesus commands his followers to love their enemies. We can love every human on the planet and still have enemies because our society is still structured in a way that gives some people unjust power over others. The best way to love our enemies is by removing them from oppressive positions and restoring their humanity through that process.

FOLLOW ME

This work of liberation includes all of us, but it is led from below, not from above. It is first named by those who experience the constraints of the current world, and the new world is developed as a solution to the problems they name. Even if we do not see the new world we desire in our lifetime, we still get the honorable opportunity to commit our short lives to this long and difficult work of liberation.

The only way we can relate to each other in healthier ways is by transforming our material conditions so that we may open up space to relate to each other in ways we couldn't have before. Religion has been used to suppress these efforts by justifying our social divisions, but religion can also be used to empower our resistance to our social divisions. This is the tension we live with. Awareness of this tension can help us intentionally choose the form of faith that truly frees us.

That's the kind of religion I'm interested in.

That's the kind of Jesus I'm interested in.

That's the kind of God I'm interested in.

That's the kind of life I'm interested in.

A life lived to the fullest is a life committed to our collective liberation. That idea drove Jesus to the cross. We can debate endlessly about what happened metaphysically when Jesus died on the cross and what it means on a cosmic level that Jesus died "for us," but we can say with absolute certainty that Jesus also died in the way most revolutionaries do. Jesus died for a cause. He wouldn't have gathered followers before his death if his death was solely for the purpose of making a metaphysical transaction in an otherworldly spiritual realm.

He died for us—all of us, right here, right now.

And we are called to respond by picking up our own crosses.

And we do that by stirring up the same kind of trouble.

CONCLUSION

In 2012, the artist Annabel Daou made a video featuring a still image of an old box-shaped television in an empty white room with a recording of the artist asking various people, "Which side are you on?" and their responses.[1] With such an abrupt and blunt question and no context, most people were taken off guard and were unsure how to respond, but they still responded. You hear in the video, "the far side," "the flip side," "God's side," "the right side," "the wrong side." You also hear people say things like, "Which side of what?" and "What do you mean, which side am I on?" and "I'm trying to figure it out." They each express a sense of uneasiness in their responses, whether they give an answer or not.

It's difficult to say which side we are on because we are often made to feel like each and every issue of injustice is too complicated to pick sides. This confusion occurs especially when the conflicts we are inundated with are interpersonal conflicts between individuals. The reason all our small interpersonal conflicts are often illuminated in the current world is because it's easier than uniting in our common struggles and building a new world that is better for all of us, not just the few in power.

If we want change in the world, then we must begin by listening to those who are most affected by the constraints of the current world. We must pray for eyes to see and ears to hear "what is upsurging from below." If we want to find God, we will only find God manifest in "the least of these." Jesus's famous parable goes:

> Then the king will say to those at his right hand, "Come, you that are blessed by my Father, inherit the kingdom prepared for you from the foundation of the world; for I was hungry and you gave me food, I was thirsty and you gave me something to drink, I was a stranger and you welcomed me, I was naked and you gave me clothing, I was sick and you took care of me, I was in prison and you visited me." Then the righteous will answer him, "Lord, when was it that we saw you hungry and gave you food, or thirsty and gave you something to drink? And when was it that we saw you a stranger and welcomed you, or naked and gave you clothing? And when was it that we saw you sick or in prison and visited you?" And the king will answer them, "Truly I tell you, just as you did it to one of the least of these who are members of my family, you did it to me."[2]

The apostle Paul continues preaching on this theme of the least of these when he says, in 1 Corinthians 1:

> Consider your own call, brothers and sisters: not many of you were wise by human standards, not many were powerful, not many were of noble birth. But God chose what is foolish in the world to shame the wise; God chose what is weak in the world to shame the strong; God chose what is low and despised in the world, things that are not, to reduce to nothing things that are, so that no one might boast in the presence of God.[3]

This is one of my favorite passages in scripture. You may be wondering if all this talk of God being on the side of the poor and powerless is suggesting that God is inaccessible to the rich and powerful. I believe God is accessible and known by all of us, no matter who we are, and not just a specific nation, or class, or even religion. However, what I love about the Christian story is that this God makes that universal accessibility possible by choosing to be manifest exclusively through the foolish, the weak, the low and despised. Not everyone has access to high and powerful places, but everyone does have access to the low and powerless places, including high and powerful people. So in order to be manifest to everyone, this God must be exclusively manifest through the low and powerless.

I'm talking about the people society disregards as not knowing what's good for them, or as not working hard enough, or as lost causes, or invaders, or leeches. That is where God is to be found: through those who are the most ostracized by society.

Furthermore, this passage in 1 Corinthians shows us that not only is this God exclusively manifest through the most vulnerable in society, but this God is also exclusively manifest through the most vulnerable parts of ourselves.

God chooses the foolish, the weak, the low and despised parts of society to appear, and chooses the foolish, the weak, the low and despised parts of ourselves to appear.

We can even say the parts of ourselves and our identities where society abuses us are the same parts of ourselves where God chooses to be made known through us. I'm talking about our vulnerabilities. We don't like to dwell on those parts of ourselves or those parts of our society. And yet, that is precisely where this God is to be found.

So when determining which side we are on, we must contemplate the most vulnerable parts of society, and the most vulnerable parts of ourselves. God is not bound in any building made by human hands. God is not even in some other metaphysical realm. God is there, manifest in those vulnerabilities.

The God who riots lurks within the vulnerable and lures us to build a new world. This process happens again and again throughout history. And as we change, God changes along with us, calling us to greater love and liberation.

ACKNOWLEDGMENTS

Love and thanks to:

My parents, for being so supportive my whole life. My commitment to curiosity and growth comes from you.

Tim Burnette and Way Collective, for being my church, committed to love and liberation.

Taylor Storey and Collin Burnett, for writing alongside me and keeping me motivated.

Kyle Kern, for being a huge inspiration and helping me focus all my ideas so I could write this book.

Casey Overton, for being so encouraging and helping me articulate who I wrote this book for.

Nick Whinnery, for being an amazing friend and motivating me to keep creating during so many life transitions.

Frank Limon, Jeff Henderson, Josh Perez, Jordan Medeiros, Stanford Midling, Chad Lamon, Chris Sanchez, Ryan McCashen, Justin Thomas, and Nik Koyama, for keeping me grounded and joyful while writing this book.

Lisa Kloskin, my editor, and the whole team at Broadleaf Books for giving me an opportunity to write this book and helping me shape it.

And my online community, which has given me joy, inspiration, wisdom, and a platform to share this book.

NOTES

INTRODUCTION

1. Luke 4:18 NRSV.
2. David Karsner, *Debs: His Authorized Life and Letters* (United States: Boni & Liveright, 1919), 48.
3. Matthew 25:40.

CHAPTER 1

1. Philippians 2:12 NRSV.
2. Acts 2:40 NRSV.
3. Acts 2:44–47 NRSV.

CHAPTER 2

1. Abraham Joshua Heschel, *God in Search of Man* (New York: Farrar, Straus & Giroux, 1955), 10–11.
2. Abraham Joshua Heschel, *The Sabbath* (New York: Farrar, Straus & Giroux, 1951), 13.
3. Luke 1:28 NRSV.
4. Origen, "Against Celsus," in *The Ante-Nicene Fathers, vol. IV: Fathers of the Third Century*, ed. Rev. Alexander Roberts, Sir James Donaldson, and Arthur Cleveland Coxe (New York: Cosimo, 1885), 408.

5. Luke 6:20–21 NRSV.
6. Passion City Church, "The Beloved Community – Dan Cathy, Lecrae, Louie Giglio," YouTube video, 1:10:37, June 15, 2020, accessed August 30, 2021, https://youtu.be/xEuI-03Jcc4/.
7. 1 Corinthians 15:22.
8. Luke 3:6.
9. Ephesians 1:23.
10. Luke 6:24–25 NRSV.
11. Michael K. Honey, *Going Down Jericho Road* (New York: W.W. Norton, 2011), 211.
12. Honey, *Jericho Road*, 298.
13. Paulo Freire, *Pedagogy of the Oppressed* (New York: Continuum Publishing, 1970; London: Penguin Books, 2017), 38.

CHAPTER 3

1. Jennifer Harvey, *Whiteness and Morality* (New York: Palgrave Macmillan, 2007), 75.
2. Indigenous Values, *Dum Diversas*, Doctrine of Discovery, July 23, 2018, accessed August 30, 2021, https://doctrineofdiscovery.org/dum-diversas/.
3. Christopher Columbus, *The Journal of Christopher Columbus*, trans. Clement R. Markham (London: Hakluyt Society, 1893), 38.
4. Indigenous Values, *Inter Caetera*, Doctrine of Discovery, July 23, 2018, accessed August 30, 2021, https://doctrineofdiscovery.org/inter-caetera/.
5. Indigenous Values, *Inter Caetera*.
6. 1 Chronicle 20:6 NRSV.
7. Robert A. Williams Jr., *Savage Anxieties* (New York: Palgrave Macmillan, 2012), Chapter 1.
8. Williams Jr., *Savage Anxieties*, 102.
9. Hal Foster, "The Art of Fetishism," *Fetishism as Cultural Discourse,* ed. Emily Apter and William Pietz (New York: Cornell University Press, 1993), 254.

10. Javier Villa-Flores, "Voices from a Living Hell," in *Local Religion in Colonial Mexico*, ed. Martin Austin Nesvig (Albuquerque: University of New Mexico Press, 2006), 236–37.

CHAPTER 4

1. Frederick Douglass, *Autobiographies* (New York: Library of America, 1994), 97.
2. Frederick Douglass, *Selected Speeches and Writings* (Chicago: Lawrence Hill, 1999), 199.
3. Douglass, *Autobiographies*, 97.
4. Luke 1:52–53.
5. Matthew 15:22–28 NRSV.
6. Collectif James Baldwin, "James Baldwin & Nikki Giovanni - A Conversation (1971) Complete," YouTube video, 1:56:38, February 28, 2019, accessed August 30, 2021, https://youtu.be/4Jc54RvDUZU/.
7. Karl W. Lampley, *A Theological Account of Nat Turner* (New York: Palgrave Macmillan, 2013), 3–4.
8. Lampley, *Nat Turner,* 123.

CHAPTER 5

1. Romans 5:20.
2. Bruce Chilton, *Rabbi Jesus* (New York: Doubleday, 2000), 110.
3. John D. Caputo, *The Weakness of God* (Bloomington: Indiana University Press, 2006), 146.
4. Richard A. Horsley, *Jesus and the Spiral of Violence* (Minneapolis: Fortress Press, 1993), 184.
5. Peter Damian, "Selections from his Letter on Divine Omnipotence," trans. Paul Vincent Spade, 1995, accessed August 30, 2021, https://pvspade.com/Logic/docs/damian .pdf.
6. Damian, Selections.

7. Damian, Selections.
8. Matthew 19:26 NRSV.
9. Caputo, *Weakness*, 224.
10. Acts 3:21.
11. Colossians 1:20.
12. Revelation 21:5.
13. Luke 15:17–19 NRSV.
14. Luke 15:20–24 NRSV.
15. Luke 15:25–32 NRSV.
16. Amos 5:23–24 NRSV.
17. Matthew 18:21–22 NRSV.
18. Luke 17:4 NRSV.

CHAPTER 6

1. Matthew 5:3, 10.
2. Matthew 8:11.
3. Mark 1:15.
4. Luke 17:21.
5. Matthew 13:31–32.
6. Matthew 13:33.
7. Matthew 6:10 NRSV.
8. Luke 4:18 NRSV.
9. Matthew 11:4–5 NRSV.
10. Matthew 20:16.
11. Frantz Fanon, *The Wretched of the Earth,* trans. Richard Philcox (New York: Grove Press, 2004), 2.
12. Critical Resistance, "What Is the Pic? What Is Abolition?" accessed August 30, 2021, http://criticalresistance.org/about/not-so-common-language/.
13. Angela Y. Davis, *Freedom Is a Constant Struggle* (Chicago: Haymarket Books, 2016), 77.
14. Angela Y. Davis, *Abolition Democracy* (New York: Seven Stories Press, 2005), 92–93.
15. Davis, *Abolition Democracy*, 92.
16. Alicia Garza, "A Herstory of the #BlackLivesMatter Movement by Alicia Garza," *The Feminist Wire*, accessed

August 30, 2021, https://thefeministwire.com/2014/10/blacklivesmatter-2/.

17. Alex S. Vitale, *The End of Policing* (Brooklyn: Verso, 2018), 2.

18. Mariame Kaba, *We Do This 'Til We Free Us* (Chicago: Haymarket Books, 2021), 2–3.

19. Miguel A. De La Torre, *Embracing Hopelessness* (Minneapolis: Fortress Press, 2017), 5.

20. Luke 1:52–53 NRSV.

21. The CR10 Publications Collective, *Abolition Now!* (Oakland: AK Press, 2008), 4.

22. Avery F. Gordon, "Some Thoughts on Haunting and Futurity," Borderlands 10, no. 2 (2011), Gale Academic OneFile, accessed August 30, 2021, https://link.gale.com/apps/doc/A276187005/AONE?u=anon~995ed35d&sid=googleScholar&xid=da3de1ba/.

23. Dan Berger, Mariame Kaba, and David Stein, "What Abolitionists Do," *Jacobin*, accessed August 30, 2021, https://www.jacobinmag.com/2017/08/prison-abolition-reform-mass-incarceration.

CHAPTER 7

1. Martin Luther King Jr., "Beyond Vietnam," The Martin Luther King, Jr. Research and Education Institute, accessed March 13, 2021, https://kinginstitute.stanford.edu/encyclopedia/beyond-vietnam/.

2. Luke 10:30–37.

3. Hugh McDonnell, "The Left Side of the Church," *Jacobin*, accessed August 30, 2021, https://www.jacobinmag.com/2018/12/church-liberation-theology-latin-america-left/.

4. Matthew 21:28–31 NRSV.

5. Darrel Enck-Wanzer, ed., *Young Lords: A Reader* (New York: New York University Press), 32.

6. Enck-Wanzer, *Young Lords,* 206.

7. Peter Rollins, "John Caputo on the Event in Christianity," YouTube video, 21:49, July 12, 2015, accessed November 22, 2021, https://youtu.be/R2nq8baHDFY.
8. 1 John 4:7–12 NRSV.
9. Marguerite Porete, *The Mirror of Simple Souls,* trans. Ellen L. Babinksy (New York: Paulist Press), 104.

CHAPTER 0

1. Acts 17:24.
2. Richard Gilman-Opalsky, *Specters of Revolt* (London: Repeater Books, 2016), 245–247.
3. Martin Luther King Jr., "Letter from Birmingham Jail," The Martin Luther King, Jr. Research and Education Institute, accessed March 13, 2021, https://kinginstitute.stanford.edu/encyclopedia/letter-birmingham-jail/.
4. Raya Dunayevskaya, *Rosa Luxemburg, Women's Liberation, and Marx's Philosophy of Revolution* (Urbana, IL: University of Illinois Press, 1991), xxvii.
5. Mark 11:2–3 NRSV.
6. Mark 11:9–10 NRSV.
7. Horsley, *Spiral*, 34.
8. Marcus J. Borg and John Dominic Crossan, *The Last Week* (New York: Harper One, 2006), 32.
9. Mark 11:15–16 NRSV.
10. Jennifer Bjorhus, "How the Fall of the Third Precinct Station Resounded in the Twin Cities," *Star Tribune,* July 28, 2020, https://www.startribune.com/how-the-fall-of-the-third-precinct-station-resounded-in-the-twin-cities/570671281/.
11. *Star Tribune*, "E-Mails, Public Records Reveal What Happened before Minneapolis' Third Precinct Was Abandoned." August 12, 2020, https://www.startribune.com/minneapolis-third-precinct-george-floyd-emails-public-records-reveal-what-happened-before-abandoned-mayor-frey/566290701/.
12. Bjorhus, "Third Precinct Station."

13. Bjorhus, "Third Precinct Station."
14. Mark 11:13–14 NRSV.
15. Borg and Crossan, *The Last Week,* 35.
16. Mark 11:17 NRSV.
17. Jeremiah 7:3–4 NRSV.
18. Jeremiah 7:5–11 NRSV.
19. CNN, "One Million Refugees and Migrants Entered Europe in 2015; Black Lives Matter Protest Scheduled at Mall of America; No White Christmas This Year; Top Ten Trending Stories of 2015," aired December 15, 2015, CNN, accessed August 30, 2021, http://archives.cnn.com/TRAN-SCRIPTS/1512/22/cnr.02.html/.
20. CNN.
21. CNN.
22. Matthew 21:14–16 NRSV.
23. Horsley, *Spiral,* 9–10.
24. Horsley, *Spiral,* 30.
25. Horsley, *Spiral,* 287.
26. Horsley, *Spiral,* 300.
27. Luke 19:41–44
28. Vicky Osterweil, *In Defense of Looting* (New York: Bold Type Books, 2020), 13.
29. Osterweil, *In Defense,* 13.
30. Kaba, *We Do This,* 2.
31. Mark 11:20–24 NRSV.
32. David M. Jacobson, "The Design of the Fortress of Herodium," *Zeitschrift Des Deutschen Palästina-Vereins (1953-),* vol. 100 (1984), 127, accessed August 30, 2021, http://www.jstor.org/stable/27931224/.

CHAPTER 9

1. Ill Will, "The Eternal Return of Revolt," July 8, 2020, accessed August 30, 2021, https://illwill.com/the-eternal-return-of-revolt/.
2. Osterweil, *In Defense,* 4.
3. Osterweil, *In Defense,* 4–5.

4. John 2:14–16 NRSV.
5. Osterweil, *In Defense*, 6.
6. Luke 23:34 NRSV.
7. Freire, *Pedagogy*, 30.

CONCLUSION

1. Annabel Daou, "Which Side Are You On?" accessed September 1, 2021, https://annabeldaou.com/Which-side-are-you-on/.
2. Matthew 25:34–40 NRSV.
3. 1 Corinthians 1:26–29 NRSV.